THE OTHER GUY

AAKASH MEHROTRA

ISBN 978-93-52019-71-7

Cover Design: Fravashi Aga
Printing: Thompson Press

First published in India in 2017 by
PLATINUM PRESS
An imprint of
LEADSTART PUBLISHING PVT LTD
Unit No. 25/26, Building A/1
Near Wadala RTO, Wadala (East)
Mumbai 400037, INDIA
T + 91 22 24046887 **F** +91 22 40700800
E info@leadstartcorp.com **W** www.leadstartcorp.com

To everyone who has been a part of this journey;
with their ideas, thoughts and stories

About the Author

AAKASH MEHROTRA is a management consultant working in the field of financial technology, using technology to extend financial services to rural and low income households. He did his masters in Forestry Management, focussing on its social applications. An environmentalist at heart and inclined towards social development, Aakash believes the market route is the way forward, as is technology to underpinning sustainable development.

He constantly travels on work and works to find the human moments in travel – experiencing myriad cultures and listening to people's deeply imbibed philosophies. His peripatetic lifestyle and love of stories, have turned him into a travel writer. Today, he is among the leading travel writers in India, widely published in the national and international media. His blog *handofcolors* is ranked among the top travel blogs.

Aakash is a theatre enthusiast, having performed in plays, short films and radio plays. Juggling data and numbers by day, he dives deep into the world of imagination by night. *The Other Guy* is his maiden attempt at fiction writing.

He can be reached at: trulyakash@gmail.com.

Contents

It is a moonless night, mysterious yet mesmerizing. The winds blow light and mercurial, gusting and howling like a child who has been admonished. It is dark, completely dark. The inky blackness carries mystery and casts a wizardly spell, to the accompaniment of the haunting hooting of an owl.

I stand on the balcony, smiling at the play nature has staged before me. The darkness is ephemeral; it will be gone when the first rays of the sun kiss the earth.

He has taken his stand. He is ready to play the game I have devised in my tortured mind. It seems the best way — a win for all. I had felt a sense of panic stepping into the trackless unmapped unknown. Yet I followed where the path led, every day; seeking an answer to the question that lay hidden somewhere in my past, perhaps unnoticed and unappreciated. It had been an agonizing decision to ask the person I loved from the depths of my soul, to marry someone else; it had the potential of taking the lifeblood from me; a decision difficult to take even under the effects of a heavy dose of drugs.

It had been a weary path. Every time I presented my logic, I could feel the deep throbbing of fear in my veins, the pain in my heart — perhaps akin to the moment before the knife descends on the sacrificial lamb. But it is the only way we can live all relationships. I will never be accepted in his life the way I am, among the people he knows. I can be friend and confidante, but not lover and life partner.

My eyes blink at the sky as if it were crowded with apparitions. My hand traces my oblivious face involuntarily. Beneath my warm fingers I can feel the shadow lurking — tormented, vandalized, haunted. There are moments that hold the potential of erasing the lines on a face with a smile that laughs at oneself. And then there are moments as black as this night, which define one's identity as darkly. Gross yet ornamented, it pulls you down yet strengthens you to regain yourself. The tears shed in the quest to know yourself wet the face but protect the soul.

This is my moment. How I have chosen will decide my future. He has another life to live; he cannot be mine alone. This is the indelible truth of my life. Yet I must strive to pull him back to me; to have him for myself.

This moment of agony will pass and I will have the chance to write the happy episode I know will come — the last chapter of my life — which will define all the decisions I have taken. It will be the great win over all my losses.

*****

1

THE INCOMPLETE MAN

He is asleep and I cannot stop looking at him. His wry smile, expressing his benevolent charm, enthralls me. His palm lies on my thigh. Unconsciously my thumb rubs against his palm, awakening my senses. My hands caress his dry, unkempt hair. My eyes have a fixed gaze. With every look I want to own him; keep him for myself. His eyeballs move, as if chasing dreams, giving me a strange feeling of comfort – the comfort of having him beside me.

It has been years with him now. And my life has undergone a grand reshaping with him – his every smile is a desire fulfilled; his lips giving my heart the loving comfort it longed for; his intense gaze melting the melancholy crouched within. Every moment with him has been cherished. I wish I could hold the moments in a handkerchief I could carry with me forever. Love has always had a different meaning for me – a burning passion with no repose, with no chances of turning back to normalcy. These bright years have passed like streaking lights in the sky, quick and ephemeral; a flash of light, then deep darkness.

He makes a deep sound, the fathomless sigh of desire as my fingers brush against his. I love his every touch. With a quick smile crossing my face, I caress his hair, bringing my palms to his cheek. He moans, slowly shedding the embrace of slumber. Bringing my open palm to his lips, he places a solemn kiss.

"You aren't asleep?" he asks drowsily, turning towards me, my palm still held to his cheek.

"No, I'm not," I reply, a germane smile on my face. I know I have every reason to feel good; he is with me, for me.

"Anything troubling you?"

I hear concern in his voice. "No, nothing in particular," I say.

"You aren't hiding something, are you? You usually have a lot going on in your mind."

"This time it is frozen. No thoughts. I have you with me today; there is no reason to feel stressed."

He gets up and comes to sit close beside me, throwing an arm over my shoulder. He smiles, looking into my eyes, as if reading my thoughts. He holds me tight, the odour of last evening's whisky still on his breath. He brings his lips to mine and kisses me – intense and intimate. His lips fret down my neck as he draws closer. Physically and emotionally my body cries for more as his lips traverse down my body to my belly. He eases me with innumerable kisses as I hold him tight, my hands caressing his back. His toned body has a feeling of fullness, like the bulge in his pants. My passionate response is my answer. He smiles at the thought of another love-making session, the third this day. I smile at the same thought, my heart declaring the perpetuity of our love.

I want him, to an undefinable extent. We have trolled along harsh stretches together, using every roughness in our favour, loving each other more. He is the answer to all the questions I have asked myself my whole life. I can go to any extent to please him. I can sacrifice anything to bring a smile to his face. Maybe sacrifice is my gift.

He whispers, "I love you."

I nod my head in acknowledgement, my answer another kiss on his lips. I want this moment to remain forever. I know he may not be there the next morning or the next night. He has his life, I know. I rest my head on his chest.

He kisses my forehead and asks, "Why do you do this to me?"

I smile innocently, choosing not to answer. He knows he will never get an answer. Every time he kisses me I feel myself sinking deeper into a dark abyss, a space full of questions. He holds me snugly and my hands rub across his chest. I love playing with his chest hair, a few of which proudly poke out from the middle of his sternum. He moves closer and my lips part to accommodate his breath.

His eyes are serious, mine full of trepidition. My tongue skims over my lips as I clasp his cheeks, my eyes glowing with the eternal brightness of love in darkness. He looks into my eyes and smiles as he places his hand on my back, a soft, seductive touch, moving down to softly hold my waist. I inhale shakily as his fingers caress my body. He bends to kiss my chest, moving his tongue over my belly before biting me softly. My legs rub against his, creating an eclectic sensation.

He does not linger but moves his lips below my belly button. My breathing and heart begin to race. I can feel the pumping of hormones enthralling me, taking me prisoner. I wilfully succumb. His hard erection presses against my body. It is such a thrill knowing I can turn him on like this. His fingers move skilfully between my thighs. As the sensations grow, I sink my head into the pillow, clenching my teeth, groaning in excitement. He takes me to a place from where it is impossible to return.

Finally he raises his face, a smile which is half-pain and half-desire on his face. "You make me fall in love again and again," he says gently.

Oh baby, I feel the same and a lot more. My burning desire converts into an inescapable fire that consumes me. I want to speak but cannot. My legs are pinioned by his. I bite my lower lip and moan in exhilaration as he stares at me… his intense gaze… *his hazel eyes*…I could never resist them. His gloating smile hangs at the corners of his lips as he kisses me again on my belly. We are caught in nature's sweet crime. It is not the first time with him but every time seems different. Perhaps it is the long wait that makes it so sensationally good.

I love him and want to scream this at the top of my voice, but all I can murmur is, "Love me".

He is over me, his lips caressing my fragile body, tantalizing me with his touch, firing me inside. I erupt with joy as he enters my body, his hips moving rhythmically. My moans grow louder, expressing the thrill of fusion. I feel his love and want drenching my soul, answering my endless questions, brightening the dark corners of my life. I close my eyes in bliss.

***

He left early. I do not know when I fell asleep but when I awoke he was gone. The last I remember was being held in his arms. He always does that, leaving early while I slept. Maybe this is how it goes – clueless love. I sometimes believe it is an unwelcome relationship. We have to live dual lives; there is no one to blame. It is we who have decided on this set-up. It will take time to get everything straight. It has not reached the stage when he can think of coming out of the shell of his past life to live and plan his present and future with me. That will change some day. At least I console myself with the promise of that thought. And if it does not, I know that in our relationship waiting is not a loss; hiding our love from others is not an escape but a necessity.

We have both made difficult choices. I did not hesitate to rebel against my family, breaking all ties with them – an adamant act. But if they cannot acknowledge who I am, why stay on? And Nikhil lives a lie devised by me. I did not wish to see his mother hurt. I have shaped our tomb.

Another morning and the struggle begins anew, to be what people wish to see me as. Hiding feelings, concealing my identity, escaping those sharp narrow looks which label you as 'different'; living an image conceived by the formal suit. In the last few days waking really hurt, a sullen feeling overcoming me. Mornings are just cold reminders of being alone, another day to drag through. It takes time to be my other self, to unclothe myself from my nightwear, in which I was me, and get into my day attire, in which I am as others perceive and define me – the unreal me who lives merrily with the world but cries alone at his loss. By the time I dress and become the sleek, polished guy in the mirror, I have donned the role I have to play the whole day.

I am gay; I sleep with my boyfriend at night and live the life of a 'straight' guy during the day. Looking into the mirror, I see myself; my predicament stares back at me. A dual life. I must live it with a smile on my face.

He has sent a message: *Sorry left so early, didn't want to disturb you in sleep, love you a lot.* I chuckle and reply: *Love you. Hope to see you soon.*

'Soon' is just another word in the dictionary for us, it has never been 'soon'. He travels 500 miles to be with me. He comes every fortnight to spend the weekend, sometimes on the pretext of a meeting in Delhi. He never has any plans, merely falling in with mine – my crazy plans – be it kite-flying near India Gate or experimenting with a new cuisine at some far-off restaurant. I always make plans to go out with him. And *chai ki chuski* at a nearby tea stall, along with a casual smoke break, has become a ritual. But I always see a certain anxiety in his smoke circles. I know he loves me but cannot show it in public; subjects better left untouched.

I check the newspaper, the same old stories of hatred, vengeance and political mud-slinging. After a brief flipping of pages I'm off to prepare lunch. I hurriedly boil some potatoes. Late night intense sex is a game-spoiler. He lies awake like an insomniac and then rushes to office at the crack of dawn while I awaken lazily, dreaming and ruining my entire work plan. I have a tight schedule and a disciplined approach to life, rather unexpected in a debonair like me. An hour of yoga sets the pace for me. He says it's good to keep in shape and he feels good about owning my toned body. A compulsory half hour is spent in cooking before I indulge after-thoughts and decisions about the day. The life of a radio jockey is messy. One's time is spent either planning a programme or broadcasting it. In my leisure time I am a freelance writer for a leading newspaper.

He has developed a ritual of listening to my poems whenever he comes. I once said to him: *You cannot have everything for free.* To which he laughed out loud. In our relationship I do most of the talking; he is the quiet listener. Three things are permanent fixtures in my life: good music, good food, and my good boy.

I have an interview today, for my weekend newspaper column. I'm supposed to meet an angel healer. I write on spirituality, giving divine comfort to my readers. I find this particularly ironic – a person so vexed from within, pacifying others. There is a psychological rule I suppose, that only those who suffer can understand the gravity of another's pain. I have always believed that when you reach the point when you cannot take the pain anymore, you start loving or living it. I keep telling myself and others who listen or read my words, not to stop loving oneself for no pain is greater than self-hate. We are all wrecking balls meant to hit and bounce back.

***

It is a summer morning and the sun is harsh at this time of year. Unexpectedly, it offers me a strange comfort today. I steel myself for the Delhi traffic. As I get into a rickshaw for the metro, my phone buzzes. It's him, messaging to wish me well for the interview. I fill with *oomph* whenever I see his messages; he loves me from the very core of his heart. He never misses even the most trivial of things. Smiling, I reply: *Thanks for being in my life.*

I reach the Metro. Twenty minutes later I change at Central Secretariat for Rajiv Chowk. People from all walks of life throng it – different colours merging into nothingness. The city has unparalleled charm – the boulevards of Connaught Place (where my office is), the unhygienic yet inviting roadside food stalls of Lajpat Market, the quaint shopping streets of Sarojini Nagar and Janpath, and the inescapable magic of Chandni Chowk, which gets more fervid and enticing as the day lengthens. Though Delhi lacks the night life of Mumbai, the joy and intimacy of Kolkata, and the intensity and grit of Bangalore, it nevertheless holds and empowers you.

I get down at Rajiv Chowk, grab a burger from McDonalds (pondering how this junk fits into my disciplined life), cast a look at the daily huddle of Palika Bazaar, giggle at the pace with which life moves and mutates people and places, and then set off to walk towards Gol Market. The strangers I meet on my way look familiar. I often wonder if they somehow know I am the RJ they tune in to listen to daily, or the person they read in O Zone every Sunday. I laugh aloud at the thought of being an unknown yet appreciated celebrity. They love me, I presume. My day starts with a sigh, a latent desire which is so potent that at times it leaves me gasping for answers, and every day I become a celebrity for millions as they tune in to listen to me saying: *Hello Dilli! Merijaan...namaskar, aadab, sasriyakaal.*

I arrive at my destination — a sprawling old building that houses the celebrated angel healer, Tanya. From childhood I have felt moved by powers that are beyond thought, perhaps beyond explanation. There will always be things we cannot hold, cannot control. I was fourteen when my elder sister asked me to join her in calling down a spirit. *Death is nothing*, she said. I did not understand then that it would help me come closer to the darker truths of life, sinister truths. My sister would say: *It is the gravity of your sins that holds you here*. Though many years have passed since then, those memories remain. Her words: *Your pain can embalm someone* still force me towards spiritual lands and resonate in my ears.

I first met Tanya in Dubai, at a spiritual workshop. She led a weird life — sullen, tranquil and stagnant. "Let the divine spark in you light. With it, grace will enter your life and a new life will begin," she told me. I was puzzled by what she said and never tried to guess what she meant. I just did not understand. But her relaxed presence helped me move on.

Wondering how a person can lead such a stagnant life so close to the shopping heart of the city, I knocked. She opened the door — a middle-aged woman with a radiant face and smile, dressed in white.

"Ah! You're here! It has been a long time," she remarks graciously. "So how are you doing? Much seems to have changed, don't you think?"

"I'm fine; not much changed," I reply with a fleeting smile.

She smiles back sceptically, eyebrows raised. *Oh Lord! It's so difficult hiding things from her*. I can count on my fingers the times we have met, yet she seems to understand me completely. She knows the real me. I had consulted her before taking the most difficult decision of my life.

She rubs my arm. Coming closer she gives me a platonic kiss. "You know why I like you? You're a fighter, a genuine fighter," she asserts.

I smirk, choosing not to answer the rhetorical question. But I wonder what she sees that is so strong about me? I bite my lip, imagining myself as a fighter. I have never sung dirges in the dark; I have only loved my life without feelings of guilt or regret, and always hated the pretence of sympathy. Did that make me brave and strong? I'm not ready for such talk today.

We get into the interview and talk about reinventing life. Finally I stand up and taking her leave, depart for the radio station. I know constant reinvention in life is the only way to help keep oneself afloat. I have always felt it was easier to say or write such things. My thoughts become mired in the smoky air of Delhi. Dust from the construction work begun long ago, still smothers passersby. It has been years since Connaught Place became cramped, barricaded and trussed up to create space for a construction project, the citizens at a loss as to what the piles of concrete and sand which block half the road and impinge on the beauty of the Circle which once personified Delhi, are for. As usual I chose to ignore the construction. Grabbing a burger from Wenger's I raced to the radio station.

Life seems simple at times — a strict work schedule to follow and endless lonely nights. Every morning I reinvent my life, but something always seems to be following me – a hangover from the past. In the silence of aloneness feelings sink in, thoughts come to shake you. Soon you seek solace in the emptiness of life and it becomes seductive, soothing, living and possessing you. The past holds and caresses you, bringing calm, astonishing trajectory of the present. But the past never really leaves us. Casting a magical net of memories, it makes us love what we once abhorred. It holds up a mirror, showing us the true self we have left behind.

Way back I chose candour over hypocrisy, deciding to fight my way out of chaos and uncomfortable silence to openness – to a simple yes or no; to express what I want, feel, desire and believe.

*****

2

ᴚIRST MEETING

I was not sure about Aarya. I never realized when and how I fell for him, or even if I ever did. He is still in touch — a good friend who knows everything. I still call him every Valentine's Day to wish him. He wishes me back — a sweet message that lifts me up for the whole day. I never thought I'd have such a person to confide in; God's gift to me.

Aarya was my roommate in the college hostel. He arrived with his parents, who helped him settle in. I too, had arrived that morning and was not yet done with arranging my clothes and other stuff when Aarya entered. Hailing from small town Gwalior, the glitz of Delhi seemed overpowering to him. And his parents carried a devastating opinion about the National capital and its folks. His mother kept murmuring: '*Dilli bada badnaam shahar hai* (Delhi is an infamous city).'

His parents stayed for three hours, enquiring about the place and the habitat, queries the CBI would have been hard put to come up with. They were afraid of the big town image of Delhi. *Dilli bada shahar hai* (Delhi is a big city)' they said over and over again. I don't know if there is such a thing as 'fear of the big city', but it was evident in their conversation and the long list of 'dos' and 'don'ts' they gave their son. They were scarcely reassured on hearing that I was a Delhi-*wallah* myself – a species they loved to hate.

Despite being a local, I had opted to stay in the hostel. After the incident with Harshit, I had quite lost my old self. I couldn't decide whether I wanted an emotional break or just to freak out. Whatever it was, I chose to stay away from my family. My mother and elder sister had guessed by then that there was something I was hiding. My sister even asked me about the change that had come over me. When I said I wanted to stay in the hostel, she helped me convince my father.

"Why do you people dream of coming to big cities if you feel so helpless to survive in them?" I asked Aarya in a tone of disgust once his parents had left.

"I understand why you ask this," he answered humbly. "See, they are my parents; they have lived their entire lives in Gwalior, so they feel protective." A smile, more bitter than complimentary, flitted across his lips as he dodged the real question.

Unlike his parents, he did not seem to carry the burden of the 'big city syndrome' and was, in fact, eager to breathe the diesel-filled air of Delhi. He threw his clothes into a corner of his wardrobe, saying cheekily, "Hope you will be able to tolerate this guy from a shanty town for three years."

"Hope you will be able to tolerate this *dilli-wala* lifelong," I replied, grinning.

He grinned back, and that marked the beginning of our friendship, which still breathes today. It took us only a few minutes to get collegial with each other. He started telling me about his fantasy relationship with his classmate. "It's better to have obsessed about someone and stalked that someone, than never to have had a crush at all," he opined, repeating the words of some novel in a reassuring tone to convince himself.

He was true. It was clear in his words, his actions, and maybe even his thoughts. Some people just click. And such relationships are worth exploring. I never thought then that this humble conversation was the start of something more enduring than many full-blooded relationships. I never imagined that I would soon become his guide to the city and we would explore this bewitching capital city of ten million people together.

He had his own plans and I was soon bombarded with questions. In a matter of days he succeeded in liberating the puzzled person within me. We grew fond of each other and his entry into my life helped me get closer to being who I really was. Aarya was impenitent about his disinterest in studies, just as he was about the way he chose to live his life. With him, I experienced moments which helped me understand myself better. A few days with him released the genie from the bottle of confusion within me. 'Has everything become alright now?' I asked myself. Surely my journey was not supposed to take such a sharp turn? My past still haunted me, its wounds unhealed. I did not feel anything as strong for Aarya as I had felt for Harshit. I admit I had grown callous after that incident.

Aarya was tall, handsome, five foot eleven, of average build and sported curly black hair. Intense eyes complemented the goofy, flirtatious smile that played at the corners of his lips. In all, he was a desirable, nay irresistible, package. His painstakingly shopped-for clothes, the new Armani fragrance he wore (and feverishly bargained for), the tower of novels he bought but never read, and his amiable smile after his ingeniously stupid acts, never failed to capture my attention. He was the mess-maker in our room and I the cleaner-up.

We went through our induction programme, perhaps the most 'religious' thing of my entire college life. Religious because we all knew we were being made sacrificial lambs. Guest lectures on the topic of media and society were real killers. Expeditions to the Delhi slums for exposure to realistic journalism proved explosive for some, making them reconsider their career aspirations. We got the hint — that media sounds glamorous but learning the tricks was a pain. We were the next 'eyes of society', as our HoD called us. Such inspirational talk boosted our morale and lifted us with the feeling of 'Oh yes!'. But soon the card house toppled before the unfolding reality of the painful exercises that went into becoming the 'eyes of society'. I do believe that the transition from one phase of life to another is always painful.

In the evenings, after continuous and strenuous classes from nine in the morning to six in the evening, we returned to our unholy shelters and bed — the only refuge for break-devoid, young seekers of knowledge. We surrendered ourselves to the sleep god, awakening only for the daily dose of calories and proteins in the college mess.

Thankfully, there were no after-dinner session planned by the seniors that night. Aarya and I sat in our room, chatting peacefully.

"Will it end some holy day?" he asked plaintively.

I stared at him questioningly. How would I know? I had not designed the seven days. "It's just the fifth day, two more days to go," I replied in a calculated tone.

Aarya looked at me, a grave look on his face, doubting my calculation. "Do you booze? I have whisky," he announced.

That came as a real surprise to me. First, it wasn't allowed, and second, it was a revelation. "I haven't tried it so far," I mumbled, hearing the guilt in my voice.

"And my parents think *you* will spoil *me*! They advised me to stay away from you!" His laughter echoed in our small room as he took a bottle of whisky from his cupboard and poured me a peg. "To our friendship!" he said, raising a toast.

I joined in…one sip, another, and then one more. A full peg went down in a matter of five minutes. I was rather too quick in gulping down the unholy drink.

Aarya stared at me, his eyes wide with astonishment. "Master of the Game!" he complimented me.

I laughed at my own innocence.

"Do you have a girlfriend?" he asked, parking his ass on the bed next to me.

I smirked and laughed off his question. The quick gulps put me completely in its control. "What about you?" I managed to ask, my head spinning. I was loving the heaviness of the drink.

He gave me a quick glance, an impish smile tugging at the corners of his lips. "My life is defined by three things: drinking, doping and anything labelled 'good-for-nothing'."

I smiled. "Is this the real you or someone who emerges only when you open a bottle?" I asked.

He giggled, pulling forward his pillow to rest his head on. "I like that girl Dhirti in our class," he said.

"Ooh…the young little tulip," I teased.

"The young tulip stands waiting in the bright light of the February sun, greeting the air, the bees, the butterflies, waiting for so long…" I said, boosting his testosterone-fed imagination. It all sounded so amusing. I had never had a sleep-over before.

He made me a second drink as I watched. "She looks cute," he said, a petulant charm to his voice.

"And all for you," I averred, raising my glass.

"So do *you* like someone?" he asked.

I wanted to say, 'Haven't yet checked out the guys'. Instead, I just smiled luxuriantly.

"You are not a true *dilli-wala*," he remarked, taking a sip.

"How do you define a true *dilli-wala*?" I asked playfully.

He looked straight at me then lowered his eyes. Bringing the glass to his lips he opined, "A true *dilli-wala* room-mate would have shared contact numbers of girls over drinks."

I looked at the sweet smile hanging at the corners of his mouth reflected in his golden drink. "You are stereotyping Delhites," I mumbled.

"I'm just giving a definition, a standard definition."

"And I am an outlier by that definition."

He smiled at my reply and got up to mix another drink. I shook my head but he continued drinking and talking at length about his life and fantasies. He had five pegs. Now I knew he had not been joking, his life *did* start and end with drinking, doping and anything labeled 'good-for-nothing'.

"Try weed some time, it gives you a high, an unparalleled feeling." Drunk, he talked about everything from girls to weeds to his virginity and missed opportunities.

I was a patient listener that night, amazed at the ease with which he shared the most personal things. And through his nonchalant talk he took me away from my old life, providing me with solutions.

Aarya took off his shirt. His fair and atheletic body with no sign of fat looked perfect in dim light. His natural, silky black hair with a hint of brown, matched his sun-kissed complexion. His perfect square jaw was a real cherry for the eyes. A moment later he took off his pants as well; I salivated in admiration. His body appeared godly, a perfect thing to be loved. I stared at the fine bulge in his underpants, trying to judge his size; pretty sure his was bigger than mine.

"Won't girls love this body?" His question distracted me.

I gave a fake smile, wanting to suggest 'not just girls'. I drooled in admiration. Dressed only in his boxers he fell onto his bed and in a matter of seconds, was snoring loudly.

Venting our hearts over drinks soon became a routine. Thanks to the super cheap liquor in Delhi, we boozed almost every night. The others in our batch remained uninvited. During the seven days of induction, we tried exploring everything forbidden in college. Aarya called it 'the real me' and I embraced this belligerence as something new and out of the routine. Those days cannot be re-lived. After induction, there was to be a Fresher's Night, thrown by the senior batches. Aarya was certain he would be crowned 'Man of the Night' and from then his 'business of darlings' would kick off. He was amusing in his own peculiar way, but also completely honest, and I admired that about him.

***

"There is some serious booty business here man," Aarya whistled, looking at twenty pairs of female legs covered only by bare necessities. It was a dream catch for him; for me there were another thirty pairs of male legs, completely covered. It was our Fresher's Night, marking the end of induction programme. For seven days we had waded through a lot of 'media and society' debate, group exercises on the cultural and ethical aspects of the media, and well-delivered guest lectures on how media not only presents society but also shapes it, gradually taking us from our casual world towards a crafted one — crafted with the intention of one day presenting the real world.

While Aarya fixed his eyes on Dhriti, I scanned the tables with their random floral decorations. Aarya had said there would be many pulsating opportunities as the three batches came together, declaring it the 'chitty-chitty bang-bang party'. I knew what he meant and looked around to map out the 'bang-bang club'.

"Hey man, you just have to get Dhirti for me," Aarya whispered as he hung an arm over my shoulder and offered me a drink with the other. "First whiskey then…" he motioned to his nether regions. "Can you arrange a place for me?"

"Not now," I remarked, popping his testosterone bubble and stepping away, my eyes searching for someone. I turned back quickly to Aarya to say, "Dhirti is alone; ask her to dance."

"Man, I'm drunk," he announced.

"Go get drunk with love then," I commanded sternly.

Helping him out seemed the only way to keep him out of my territory. I agreed to his plea that I approach Dhirti for a dance and then excuse myself and bring him in to take my place.

Dhirti stood in a corner, a soft drink in her hand. "Hi! I'm Anuj, your batch-mate," I introduced myself. She threw me a quick smile. "I saw you standing alone, so thought I'd say a quick hi." I gave her my trademark smile, which Aarya said was as saleable as Armani. She seemed to buy it. "So where are you from?" I asked.

"Chandigarh. And you're from Delhi? Yeah, I remember you introducing yourself in class." She was really graceful, a real *Punjabi pataka* as my roomie would have said unblushingly.

"You know you have an accent; funny but pristine," she said as she took a sip of her drink.

I gave her an appreciative smile. "So have you been to Delhi before? You don't seem to have many friends." I tried to take the conversation forward. Was it always so difficult to initiate a conversation with a girl?

"Yeah! I don't open up easily and no one has come up to me till now," she said, her tone acrid.

I looked her over from head to toe; she was elegant.

"What?" she asked, stiffening defensively.

"Oh I was just checking out where the label saying 'stay away' was stamped on your body since no sane man has come to talk to you," I replied.

She burst into laughter. I wondered whether my joke was really good or she was just trying to be nice to me; the former being more acceptable, though the latter would have brought a smile to Aarya's face.

"Well I came and you can certainly open up to me." I gave her my Armani smile. She smiled back shyly. From the corner of my eye I could see her interest; from the corner of her eye she might have guessed my reluctance.

"You know what, I can hardly hear you above the music so either you need to increase your volume or we go out and talk," she suggested as loudly as she dared.

"Going out seems the easier option," I yelled.

"Fine but just excuse me for a sec while I put down this glass somewhere."

"I'll get something for us to eat."

***

"The music is so loud it almost deafened me," she grumbled as we walked out of the hall.

"It is meant to serve a different purpose."

We found a couch in the reception area and sat down. The place was a percussion of light and shadow. The heavy chandelier in the centre added to the soothing appeal. I looked at her and noticed she was wearing a black suit and diamond earrings.

"So how do you like Delhi?" I asked, the simplest question I could think of to start the conversation.

"Actually I come to Delhi quite often as my grandmother lives here. But I've never explored the city in any depth. I mean I've been to most of the historical monuments, but only as a casual tourist. There is so much more I'd like to explore."

I nodded, anticipating a tiresomely lengthy travel account. Contrary to my expectation, she fell silent. "Everyone comes to Delhi with different expectations. It has turned into a city of iconoclasts," I said, sounding like a pompous oaf.

"That is true of every urban centre in the country. It has been over a decade since we opened the doors of our economy and the country is expanding without plan or preparation."

"You are still in induction mode, it seems," I joked lamely.

"You're laughing at me, but it's good to be in a field where the main requirement is perspective. And mind you, I didn't say different perspective." Her smile blended sarcasm and wit.

"I'll second that. You say what nobody says as the fourth, and supposedly unshakeable, pillar of democracy, and there may be few to hear you."

"Anuj, what really pisses me off is when people talk about media and philosophy. They ignore that in today's society, fact is fashioned as fiction and fiction is presented as fact. There is an obvious schism between the known and the told," she said, taking our innocuous discussion into high decibel territory.

"You seem to have already graduated while the others are still surviving the shock of induction," I joked, privately much impressed by her intellect.

"It wasn't 'shock' exactly. The media study imparted was not half as engaging as the word itself," she retorted, turning her head away.

"You seem to hold strong ideas," I commented.

She chose to smile. Our discussion continued, my ideas vague, hers strong and clearly presented, making ideas sound like opinions. In my head I had a picture of Aarya grinning helplessly in some corner, watching surreptitiously. I remembered Dhirti's words about perspective, and thought of cautioning my friend about the dangerously intellectual species he was dreaming of being with.

"Would you like to dance?" I asked, remembering the party and loud music, and above all the motive for my being with her. It was not the moment for deep discussion.

"Frankly, I've hardly danced in my life," she swallowed, dropping her eyes.

"Well that's the fun part; you don't have to really dance, just keep tapping your feet and in a minute you will be making moves," I said reassuringly.

"You seem quite the party animal," she replied, rolling her eyes but keeping her voice calm.

"You have three years to get to know me, but we'll have few occasions to dance together to such loud music. So let's not miss the chance!"

"After you," she said, smiling in agreement.

We proceeded to the dance floor. I had asked Aarya to approach me when he saw us head there. That was the first part of the plan, the second being for me to depart. Accordingly, Aarya came over and I awkwardly excused myself, leaving them together. I turned to look at Dhriti; she was giving me a 'You dog!' look.

That is how the three of us met. Dhriti and Aarya are married today and we remain the best of friends. And Dhriti has long known why I took no interest in her that night.

***

That evening at the party I was looking for somebody in particular. My eyes sought a face lit by short bursts of laughter, dimples in both cheeks and hazel eyes. That was enough for me to imagine he had the same devastating effect on all life on campus. He was ethereal. His eyes seemed to hypnotize. I finally located him through a glass of wine, the silver liquid the perfect foil. I was born to like him, more with every glance.

My life was like the sensex, with sudden highs and lows. Falling for the wrong person was a mistake I seemed prone to. I fertilized right ideas to win the wrong person in my mind and began living lies and rejected truths branding them as lies. And here I was preparing my mind to repeat the same mistake. Pulling myself up I looked around for my lovebirds — they were having an intense discussion in a corner. Shoulders hunched, faces turned towards each other, they sported smiles and serious expressions alternately. Good. I thought about getting something to eat, giving myself something to do besides thinking about these two men. Almost all the food was gone, except for some carrots and unwanted mushroom delights (don't know why they have such an obviously unsuitable name). Burnt-out cigarette butts lay like a bonus dish. I was left doing my thing — looking helplessly at the unsavoury options like a kid being offered leftovers.

"You want something to eat?" someone asked.

I turned. It was him...*bum bum BUMM!* He smiled, wearing cuteness like a shirt specially made for him.

"Actually, I was looking for some starters, but there aren't any left," I said shyly, like a new kid in town.

"Well you can have some from my plate and then dinner," he offered smiling, probably at my childishness.

"Thank you. By the way, I'm Anuj."

"Hi! I'm Nikhil."

"Let me get you a drink," I said. Now that sounded overtly friendly, rather funny actually, something destined to get funnier with nostalgic repetition. I smiled to hide how distractingly gorgeous he was, in a 'rich guy' way. As I mixed scotch and water, the gleam in his eye told me it's a real man's choice.

He proved a good companion with his infectious smile, awful puns, and gleaming eyes. He refilled my drink without my having to ask. He claimed me so easily, planting an unseen flag on me stating his ownership.

That night I tossed and turned, rolling over and pounding my innocent pillow. The second chapter of my love life had begun with another set of uncomfortable, unpredictable and unwelcome situations. Sighing, I hugged the pillow I had just beaten, determined to erase those incredibly attractive hazel eyes from my dreams. But I knew that wasn't possible. I was scarred for life, burnt by their beauty.

***

"Here you go! All this is for you, Aarya," I announced as I entered with a pile of books from the library.

"Hey dude!" Aarya recoiled, awe and shock in his voice.

"You wanna win Dhriti? Then try to be the guy she likes," I advised as I placed the books on his desk, laden with everything that should not have been there.

He looked at me with surprise and trepidation. "But why do I need these books, these novels?"

"So that you can have an intelligent conversation with her," I answered, a mischievous gleam in my eyes.

He looked at me, then at the novels, and then at me again. Finally he asked, "Are there any books on sex?"

I answered with an obviously fake smile, "I believe sex is just a natural act." He gave me a surprised look. "With these novels and self-help books, you will be able to converse with her."

"Ah! I believe striking up a conversation is natural too…like sex," he said unctuously. "By the time I've read all these books, she will be dating someone else."

"Who says you have to finish them before having a conversation? Both can happen simultaneously. Reading is important to get an emotional connect." I really wanted him to understand he was dealing with a highly intellectual species.

"Alright…if you say so. I'll try reading a few. I have loads of book myself which just add to the junk in our room," he replied disinterestedly as he stood up and took off his shirt to get into his night clothes.

His virile curves and well-toned body with its streak of hair starting from his navel and branching at his chest to encircle his dark nipples did its best to entice me. The jockey shorts revealed his full, beautiful buttocks. I lowered my eyes, smiling at the thought of seeing this virtual delight every night for the next three years. I felt the blood thud in my temples. He taught me the power of hormones. He looked as seductive as a tree shedding its leaves in autumn, and as naïve as a bud ready to bloom after being kissed by the sun in spring. His nightly changing ritual always inspired deeply private and corrupt thoughts.

I added water to the whiskey Aarya had poured us. Boozing had by then become almost the most pious act for us. We were in our personal paradise.

"We drink whiskey like it was water," I cheekily confessed.

He smiled back. "It will help me stay awake so I can read one of those novels."

"Are you really serious about Dhriti?" I asked.

He looked at me, his eyes bright, trying to hide a smile. He blinked, took a sip and then said, "Too much curiosity kills. Yes, I think I am," he said softly.

I saw honest vulnerability in his eyes, perhaps for the first time since we met. I couldn't quite measure the seriousness, perhaps because of the whiskey.

Aarya always slept soundly and deeply. Even today I wonder how he manages to decorate his life so well with random pieces of joy and lead such an intense yet quiet life. He could always bring order to his chaotic life, taking him closer to the consummation of his heart's desire. He was adept at straightening and arranging odds and evens. In three years of college we experienced moments when things looked like breaking and a haunting screech sounded. But he always found a reason to stay balanced. Soon our friendship alchemized into a valuable bond. We were more than friends; we were not soul-mates but soul-keepers.

***

Time is relative. As it moved willfully, I obeyed its every rule. Aarya had become my emotional booster. Nikhil, a batch senior to us, was my cup of steroids. In a matter of days, both men had created great open spaces for themselves in my life. Behind every gay is the great desire to be with an awesomely straight man. It's like the Holy Grail, a sweet escape from the reality we hide in our hearts. It is something desired and yearned for. It validates our sexuality, making us seem versatile. Acting straight is easy. It is also an aversion to being termed *femme*, and a simple route to acceptance.

For me it was definitely the last, avoiding the real me to be in a world where I would be accepted. Even years later, things have not changed. Most gays are still jocks, straight-looking guys. Let alone society, it is often difficult for us to accept ourselves as we are. People readily wear masks, locking their thoughts in a safe to which only they have the key. It is easy to act. None of my friends ever knew until I told them. It may seem that we are embarrassed by our true identity. Perhaps so, but it is the way to exist in a wider, quintessentially *normal* society; an escape from questions and forced views.

I cannot wear my sexuality on my t-shirt or sing it in my prayers — society is not open to it. I have heard my straight friends cracking gay jokes, infusing raunchy humour into their conversations. It felt like an attack on my own sexuality, but I needed them to think I was cool. I needed that. I couldn't have opened up to either Aarya or Nikhil, for they were stamped as straight guys. Still I chose to remain close to them, living my sexual dynamics in stolen glances.

With Nikhil I had to find excuses to be in his room, like needing notes or study material. After a while it became usual for me to be there, staring at him lustfully as he undressed, conniving secret plans to get closer. While talking to him I always had undertones of desire. And as the days passed, it became more and more difficult to resist.

To get closer to him I began making notes about his daily activities so I could 'accidentally' bump into him, be it going to the library or to the mess for a late dinner. I noted the things Nikhil never failed to do — play tennis every evening (he was the best in college), go for a swim every weekend, and go to hear *quawali* in the old city. I developed a matrix of all he did and what I could do. Tennis was the first tick for me. Going to the old city for food was fine but *quawali* was a big no. The easiest seemed tennis but the thought of going for a swim with him made my heart do a flip-flop. I inserted a column in the matrix labeled 'My interest' and put two ticks below swimming. I would start with these two activities. That was Plan A. Plan B, getting him interested in me, seemed a pipe dream best left in utopia.

I followed him to know everything about him. It was simple. I kept a notebook and pencil in my bag and these trustworthy friends never failed me. For a whole week I gathered information from every source I could think of, observing him closely, studying his psyche, detailing his list of friends and developing a complete map of his daily schedule. He had become a live research project for me. I put into practice every investigation technique we had learnt in class. And I noted every damn detail. I wrote down my observations; I studied his gait to analyse his personality; I recorded his voice to study modulations and mood swings. From my fixed seat on the balcony, I noted every time he went out and when he returned. I moulded our conversations to his likes and dislikes. At times I followed him, to know where he went. In short, I employed every tool possible to prepare a complete profile of my target.

Certain things emerged clearly, providing me with much needed momentum to keep conniving to get him. Most importantly, I started getting a hunch that he too, was one of the secret minority in so called straight society.

*****

3

ＤＩRTY SUNDAY

Ｓundays are good for many reasons. For me it was for the spicy chicken sandwiches the cafeteria served on Sundays and the evening bus ride from the hostel to the centre of the city, and from there to my home. But that particular Sunday was special, for I planned to put an end to my twisted infatuation. I had planned on a swim at the same pool Nikhil used. I set my watch to his and enrolled in the same batch – two hours in the pool.

My heart pounded for the whole hour and twenty minutes it took to get there. I was early. Finally I saw him come in, dressed in swimming trunks, his fair body glistening. Ever since I had first seen him, not a day passed without my thinking of him in short pants. I lived for those moments, those guilty pleasures, the little secret I had stashed away in a wild corner of my mind. And lo! Here he was coming towards me in shorts!

I waved and closed in to greet my target. "Hi! I didn't know you come here too," I remarked off-handedly.

"I've been coming here for months now, every Sunday, but I'm seeing you here for the first time." He landed a playful punch on my belly.

"Oh I was in the evening batch. It's my first time in the

morning and it's great to have company," I said chirpily, failing miserably to hide my intentions.

"What are we waiting for? Let's get in and see who is better," he replied, placing a hand on my shoulder.

A fine dive into the pool of ecstasy; he looked so desirable as his muscles flexed. My twisted infatuation slowly grew into a fatal obsession.

"As a matter of fact, our tastes seem to match. I hear you play tennis as well," I casually mentioned.

"Wow! You play tennis too? Very few in college do. I will be delighted if you prove to be a good player."

"I don't know how well I play, but I'm ready to learn from you. You played at state level if I'm not wrong."

"You seem to have gathered a lot of information about me," he joked. "Come for a tennis match one day."

"How about this evening?" I suggested.

He nodded in his typical way before diving in again, this time heading down the pool with a beautiful butterfly stroke. I was left thinking how he would be in bed — a clichéd corporate guy with logic for every position, or an artist, with poise and passion, or a smart guy who would compose music with his moves. Ah! I knew he would be the third.

The way his back muscles grew taut, the way the water glistened over his chest and abs, the way he towelled his hair dry, all sent shivers through my body. I pleaded with my heart to be still. I wanted to spend another hour with him, to find and know each other, to tell him 'you are mine.'

"So are you heading back to college from here?" he asked fingering his hair after a quick shower.

My eyes tried to capture every detail of his body, including the small mark on the right side of his back. I forced my tongue to speak. "Yeah…to college, and you?" Never in my life had I yearned to get down to the nasty. He was irresistible. If ever I was to lose myself to someone, it had to be him.

"I'm going back to college too," he said. "Let's go together; I have a bike."

Oosh! I had been waiting to hear that. An ecstatic smile crossed my face. I noticed he had uneven ears, one dimple and deep set eyes. "You know we could try some *kachoris* on the way. I know a place, a hole in the wall but it serves delicious *kachoris*," I suggested.

"You sound like quite a foodie. Let's try that too. And we must stop at a magazine counter; I want something to read."

The anti-climactic remark ruined the culinary lift I had given myself. But okay, he was into reading, discernible from the pile of books he had in his room and the orderly way he arranged his notes. Intellectual men are quite a turn-on.

"Let's go then," he said, patting me on the back.

I loved the way he walked. There was an effortless ease which commanded attention. He went ahead to get the bike from the parking lot, leaving me to dive further into my pool of desire. I prepared myself for a joyride on his Pulsar, definitely a male thing. It would be exciting to be in a harmless situation, clinging to him, oblivious of the world while he drove us out of this urban madness. I waited under a tree for ten minutes, lost in naughty thoughts.

He finally came, riding his guy machine. An effortless kick and we were off with a roar. I was in a state of total surrender. We halted to have *kachoris*, buy magazines and share jokes. I enjoyed talking to people, making new friends, but with him I was not functioning or speaking well. He did most of the talking, my role being limited to answering questions. I was both tongue and eye tied; both senses temporarily dysfunctional, one failing to work, the other concentrating only on him. I listened when he spoke, I laughed when he laughed. I flushed, feeling him so close to me.

Nikhil suggested coffee. Just one word but it made my subconscious goddess jump, jive and hop about. The day now was not just about dirty thoughts but also eventful. We stopped in front of The Café, one of the most visited youngster haunts. Seating ourselves on a small sofa by the wall, he flipped open the menu and began to scan the items.

"What would you like to have?"

A waiter who looked too young and tender to be taking orders, stopped at our table.

"We're still deciding," I said, pasting a 'so many choices it's difficult to pick one' look on my face.

Nikhil passed the menu to me, asking me to decide. I ordered at random, feeling helpless and uncertain. Trying something new always gave one an out if the dish was bad. If it turned out well, one earned the reputation of being a 'food experimenter'. I was like Hamlet: To be or not to be. Perhaps 'not to be' was the easier choice.

And soon the crepés arrived at our table, the sweet aroma of strawberry and banana assailing our nostrils.

"Ah! It smells good!" Nikhil exclaimed. "If my taste desires had a tongue, they would surely have named this dish Divine."

I wanted to tell him the dish was called crepés and he needn't stress over naming it but all I did was smile, my secret little weapon, humbly acknowledging his appreciation. I secretly plumed myself on a successful experiment.

"So I'll come by this evening for a tennis match," I said, breaking the silence that had crept in between us.

"Sure, I'll be glad to see you. I haven't seen anyone from your batch at the courts."

"Hmm…I don't think anyone plays. I don't consider myself great either but regular practice will get the best out of me," I said, sounding more confident than I felt.

Ignoring my bravado he devoured his crepé. A guy with a sweet-tooth I concluded. *Another point noted.*

"You have a sweet tooth." I tend to say what's on my mind.

He smiled his retro smile and asked, "Don't you?"

"To a limited extent."

"The word 'limited' constitutes a serious flaw in definition," he remarked, happy and busy as a bumblebee.

"It's so difficult talking with people in this college, they outsmart you constantly!" I said, flexing my hands, trying to make him feel important.

"You are quite strange. Sometimes you appear like a guy who has refused to come out of a child's skin. Remember how you were looking at the food at the freshers' party? Like a kid!"

Oh! He remembered our first meeting.

I was fat with love, grown obese with an untutored, unspoken, unfulfilled love. Everything seemed like it would turn out fine, like a nice story or a long conversation over dinner. Optimism grew every time his eyes met mine. I felt his eyes explore me, as if trying to read something hidden. I wished he would explore the same things I did in him.

"And what's so wrong with that?" I know it was a ridiculous reposté but something had to be said.

"Nothing…you just looked such a kid. Anyway, I hope to see you every Sunday for a swim. We could go together."

And that was exactly what I had been steering myself to say. I needed to pinch myself as I sat like a dubious dessert.

"Sure… and every evening for tennis."

"Wow! You seem just the person I've been looking for – sport, food *and* company."

I must have consumed lots of extra calories on hearing this.

"So the plan stands."

"It does."

***

Evening wended her way across the sky as I eagerly awaited her. I picked up a tennis racquet from the sports room and made my way towards the tennis court. It was a game few played in our college but which he was a champion at. He was there practicing his serves alone. His fair square-jawed face and hazel eyes were always a treat for me. The best thing was that he was single. With singles, their sexuality remains unknown. I had read in a medical journal that about 10 percent of males are born gay and more are now opening up to experimenting with their sexuality. I wondered if Nikhil belonged to this club.

"Should I come in?" I shouted.

"Ah! I was waiting for you. Cool that you've came. Take that side, this is my favourite."

"Are there some lucky cherries for you on that end?" I asked cheekily.

He laughed, throwing back his head. "You can think so. This is my winning side."

"As if you have any competition," I remarked morosely. "With my first serve you'll laugh in comic relief."

I played my first serve; an easy one. I missed his powerful return and he scored the first point.

"Tennis is a game of serves. If you learn that well, you get the edge," Nikhil said.

I tried again, resulting in a double fault. I looked at him guiltily.

"Let me show you," he said, crossing to my side of the court. "First, fix your gaze, then bend to begin your serve."

As I bent, bouncing the ball, he held me firmly, his hands on my pelvis, correcting my posture, his body pressed against mine as he gave instructions. I could smell the cardamom he had chewed. He brought one hand over mine, telling me to bounce the ball for the serve. I wanted to freeze that moment forever. The soft breeze carrying the fresh smell of rain had its own poetry. The rustle of the leaves seemed to share living anecdotes. In the fading orange light his face glowed. A few drops of rain, like tiny diamonds, twinkled in his hair.

"Damn! It's raining," he exclaimed, easing away from me.

"It's just a drizzle, we can continue," I suggested, giving obvious expression to having him close to me.

"Hmm…serve. Let's see how you do."

I hid a smile as I bent. Three bounces, then I threw the ball into the air and bent my body backwards… within milliseconds the flying dot had crossed the net and landed on the other side. Perfectly done by my standards; practically flawless.

"Uhmm…that's good. You've got pace and length, the only thing you need to take care of is your posture. The whole action follows a parabolic curve, a 115 degree bend and *shoo*… the ball goes. Bring more finesse to your posture and the game will get easier."

I took another ball and served again, taking into account every bit of advice he had doled out. He seemed pleased; at least his smile seemed to suggest that. "Hey, why don't you serve and show me?" I suggested.

He took a ball from me and I moved aside to watch him serve. Three bounces and then came a master *wham* – an unchallenged ace. Then again – three bounces of the ball, a parabolic turn of the body, eyes fixed, hands stretched, and *wham!* He grinned.

I ran to give him a light hug, uttering "Perfect!"

"I hope you can now do a good serve," he replied, his words a sugary treat in the wet weather.

The steady murmur of falling rain echoed gently around us. It had changed from a soft drizzle to a soothing downpour, breaking the spell of heat and dust. Dark clouds hung on the horizon and the somber stillness was animated by sudden flashes of lightning. I reached up my hands to catch some raindrops. In time to come I would often decorate my memory shelf with that hour – we stood soaked, looking into each other's eyes and laughing.

Breaking the silence he asked, "Would you like some tea?"

I wouldn't have dreamt of refusing. He got his bike from the stand and I hopped on behind, a hand on his shoulder.

"You play well," I said inanely.

He laughter rang above the thunder and rain. "I want you to play well too; I don't have much competition here. Nobody seems to play tennis."

We arrived at the students' beloved haunt – the tea stall.

"Want some *pakoras*?" I asked, ordering two cups of tea.

"Yes, it's a must-have here," he replied enthusiastically.

No one can challenge the magic of *chai-pakoda* in the first monsoon rain I thought as I put the tea cups down on the seat of the bike.

"So where are you from?" I asked.

"Lucknow, capital of Uttar Pradesh," he replied.

"My geography is better than my tennis," I assured him smiling before biting into a crispy *pakora*.

"Why did you decide to take Mass-Com?" he asked.

"I could have never made it into a good engineering college and I'm a compulsive writer," I answered. Another *pakora* went down like a dream.

"Hmmm…I was charmed by the razzmatazz of the media, so I made it here without giving it a second thought." His voice was just audible above the rain.

"Well I don't know what exactly made me decide on this course, but I think this is the best way I can be of some use."

"That thought never crossed my mind," he remarked, turning towards me. "So…any girlfriend?" The question was like an unexpected bouncer.

"Do I look like someone who has one? If I had, I would be dating her instead of having tea with you," I joked. He grinned.

"What about you, single or ready to mingle?" I asked, holding my breath.

"I don't wanna throw your answer back at you but we're both *venga* boys. I never wanted to be in a relationship. I find it just too tiring."

"But you must have had opportunities; you're impossibly handsome." My eyes had said that innumerable times already.

"You're a flatterer."

"I'd rather master the art of making people melt over my good looks," I replied with absolute honesty.

"I'm like the spoilt brat who goes to school only to pluck raw mangoes from the trees," he said cheekily. "But why should one even give a damn?" he added, his tone changing

"Yeah, you don't have to be always good to people."

It was raining heavily now, the sky dark and thundery. Having finished the last sip of my tea, I changed the topic to say, "It's now on you to teach me to play well. I'll keep bugging you."

He smiled at my enthusiasm. "Would you like to share a *dosa?*" he asked, pointing to the south Indian outlet two shops away.

"Cool! *Dosas* are delicious."

He went across to the booth and returned with a serving of *dosa* and steaming *rasam* and *sambhar*. It looked irresistible.

"I love south Indian cuisine," I announced as we ate.

"You know why *dosa* tastes great with *sambh*ar but not with chicken curry etc?"

Now I regard that a sad question. I mean, who questions the obvious? I managed to say, "It's just the perfect combination, the right thing goes with the right stuff, like you and tennis, or our tastes, which match." I marvelled at my own logic and eloquence.

Nikhil seemed to chew on my answer before nodding agreement. He would normally never have let such a careless remark pass. I got the impression that the winds of caution could change any time to chase me instead.

"Why do you think that is so?" I asked. Deep inside I wanted to change the silly topic to something more personal.

"It's as you say, mixing of the right stuff – the restraint in the spices of the *sambhar* and the blandness of the *dosa* mingle well. It's the restraint that spells magic, a welcome wait before the spice, complementing each other."

Thanks to the heavy downpour, we chatted for an hour. Every minute made me more aware of my own sexuality. Not that I did not know I was gay, but I had always tried hiding from this fact. Before opening myself to the world, I needed to open up to myself. What if Nikhil came to know? Or Aarya, the room-mate and friend I had always hoped for? These thoughts troubled me.

The only thing wrong with being gay is how people treat you. I have lived my life expecting acceptance but knowing I will not always get it. I can take tolerance over hatred, but then who wants to be just tolerated? For gays the world is too small, it calls for intestinal fortitude to digest everything. I, and everyone else for that matter, do not wish to feel we are on the wrong planet.

The question wasn't just about tolerating people's attitude towards me; it was about opening up to Nikhil. I had fallen for him the first day I saw him, and had been thinking about him ever since. I dreamt of him holding and kissing me. I knew I wouldn't be able to hold myself back from opening up to him. My introvert soul wished to be swallowed whole. I burned with desire. There were destined to be more tennis sessions, longer chats, dances in the rain, more eat-outs – I felt drunk on testosterone, thinking of it all. And I had no idea how to tell him. I felt like a guy waiting for someone on the wrong side of the tracks.

***

"Are you…?"

Harshit's words ruptured me. I looked at him, tears filling my eyes. I nodded, turning away. I loved him but at that moment I felt shattered, bewitched and helpless. I threw myself into his arms and cried. I was facing myself more than I was facing him. I had never explored my sexuality to this extent. I had been a coward. I wept my heart out.

He stood still, not saying anything. I imagined him drawing back, moving away from me, his face turned away.

"Yes I am," I revealed, gaining courage, a storm rising within me.

"I guessed it." There was stiffness in his voice.

Why had he come if he knew? Why had he come if he had nothing for me? I had no answers. Perhaps he still considered us friends. The word 'friend' pierced me like a dagger. His awkwardness explained why some relationships refuse to breathe. I knew I had to tame this insanity before it became wild and unmanageable. But I couldn't hold myself back. I failed to see the lack of love in his eyes when I had lived him every moment, day and night.

"Are you…" my voice broke. I could feel an arrow piercing me. I did not want my love to be an intrusion in someone's life. His question had cracked open the wounds of my heart. It was so difficult to love someone of one's own sex, accompanied by guilt and remorse.

Harshit did not utter a word. I sensed the 'no' in his eyes. I wasn't sure how to take things forward. Relationships between people of the same sex are not accepted. I had lived every tremour of pleasure knowing I would have to pay with an equal measure of pain. The discomfort in his eyes when I took his hand in mine was palpable, but I ignored it. His fingers were cold but touching him soothed the fumble and rush of this unfamiliar love. He would hold me, joke, lie with his arms across my body or hug me – all gestures of friendship. They brought him closer to me but not me to him.

The church bell clanged. The loud cry of kites hovering in the sky filled the silence. They seemed to know something was dying. I sat motionless as a corpse, trying to find answers in his eyes. There were none I wanted to believe. I came face to face with what made me so different. I had not expected him to accept me. I had questioned myself long before I ever met Harshit.

"It'll be okay; you're still young."

His words infected me. 'Okay'…the word echoed in my mind. It still does. What was wrong that it would become 'okay'? I was born this way. The dark sky cast its ghastly cloak over me as I sat like a lost soldier in his first battle. I sat on the steps of the church as life changed, leading from nowhere to nowhere. I sat like an absurd, neglected, weather-beaten sculpture, left to the mercy of the wild.

I looked up as 'okay' echoed in my mind again, sending a chill through me. Some things come with their own punishments, small pleasures wrapped in pain. I was gay and had to learn to abhor the ugly face of sympathy and live with conditional acceptance. What I felt was not a crime but unacceptable nevertheless…taboo…accompanied by the constant mewl of disapproval.

Harshit smiled. "Hey! Don't take it so seriously. We're still not at that ripe age to know ourselves fully. People change with time."

"Don't tell anyone," I pleaded, wiping the tears from my face.

"No way! I understand it's a difficult thing. Don't worry."

"You think ill of me…"

"You are the most innocent person I have met in my life," he said casually, as if nothing had happened. "The cutest as well, I must add. I've always loved being with you. I'm not a person who wants to get very close to anyone; but that happened with you."

"Can we still be friends?" I asked. How hard it was to extinguish the flame of hope!

"Could you be?"

His words were a dagger digging deep into my wounds. Could I be? Had I ever been able to? The same questions that often stared at me with ghostly eyes. I could not…

I lost him. He was gone. I was left alone, my cheeks still wet with tears. I wished desperately to be like others, not different in a uni-oriented world. The silver moon shone, making luminous tracks through the dark alleys of my being, hurting me with its pristine light. I wished I could drown in its silver splendour and become another soul, living another life in a different world. I felt shattered and alone…with no place to take refuge.

It was the end of a chapter of my life. I knew I would live others as painful, or better, than what I had known before.

*****

4

COFFEE AND CONVERSATIONS

I was lost in thought when the door squeaked open. It was Aarya; I could tell by his heavy gait. He sat down on the edge of his bed and scowled, tense and uptight. Another failed attempt to start a conversation with Dhriti, I guessed.

"No drinks today; I'm out of pocket money," he lamented.

"We could get some from Suraj next door but I'm okay about a whiskey fast today," I said, changing into my boxers.

"Fuck it, man! Fasting seems the better option today." He ran his fingers through his messy dark hair

"Something wrong? Wanna tell me?" I asked.

"Cannot get that girl off my mind!"

"Why do you think she does not take to you? You'll have to give her some time to get to know you. It's a matter of trust. She's from a small town; she won't melt at your looks and start palpating. Try finding what interests her."

"You can help. She considers you a bloody good friend. You know I can literally run through girls every day of the week. My face tells them not to take me seriously or expect anything more than a good time. But you, on the other hand, you have a deceptively innocent face. Now, can you set this broth on fire for me?" Aarya asked, shaking me.

Words failed me as we looked at each other, he in the grip of frustration, I blankly.

"You really need a whiskey," I said finally.

"Hey buddy, you know you can do it," Aarya urged. "See, it's real love. I know you don't wanna see your friend sitting in some corner all alone, living a life of coagulated dreams. It's not about three days but three years. I don't want my breath to hurt, my eyes to burn and my heart to bleed anymore. And I'm sure you don't want that either."

His pained tone haunted me momentarily. I took a deep breath and said, "That's what I've been trying to tell you, it's three years, give it some time."

"Look at me! Do you think it's possible? See the impatience in my eyes!"

Left with no option, I reluctantly agreed to help him. "Okay, I'll ask her out for a meal or shopping, this weekend; you can come along."

This seemed like a plan to avoid further pleadings rather than to get her close to my hero. But Aarya was overjoyed, so much so that he planted a soft kiss on each of my palms. "Hey man, I'm going to get some whiskey from Suraj," he happily chirped.

I shrugged in dismay. Whiskey seemed the answer to everything for him. Perhaps the Delhi Government ought to consider increasing the excise duty on liquor; that would save both me and my wallet.

"You know…" These opening words were enough to prepare me for some drunken philosophy from Aarya. "I know love is a very heavy word, but I…I *want* to take on the burden. I mean, I *want* this to happen. I feel different, buddy; something I've never felt before. It could be desperation or infatuation, but it is *something*."

"Have you ever slept with a girl?" I asked candidly.

"I've never even kissed a girl, forget sleeping with her," came the prompt reply and ingenuous grin.

Frankly, the revelation surprised me.

"Tell me about you, Anuj. Never felt anything for any girl?"

"Nope, never, and I don't think I ever will."

"Are you normal?" Aarya asked directly.

I sat transfixed, unable to gauge what he would say next. "How do you define normality?" I finally asked, my heart thudding.

"Normal guys like girls at this age. And since you don't get aroused on seeing those dark eyes…" He took a gulp of his whiskey. "Man, you are not normal."

I shrugged my shoulders. "It hardly matters. You do what you think is right…like drinking whiskey in the silvery night."

After a brief silence the curious kid in him rose again and he shot a volley of questions at me. "Hey, tell me man, do you really not feel anything for girls? Do you feel it for guys?"

I looked at him seriously; not annoyed. He looked straight into my eyes, probably understanding I would not answer.

"Do you feel something for me?" he asked.

I wanted to cry 'yes!', but merely flickered an indulgent smile towards him. He got back to making drinks. I wondered how best I could answer his questions.

"See, you are still thinking about me," he accused, offering me a glass.

I didn't react, just kept smiling. Did he somehow know? Had I been too obvious when I looked at him changing? Had I got closer to him than what could be defined as normal? Something must have prompted him to question me.

We sat gulping down our drinks. The sensitive topic soon evaporated and Aarya was back to defining love. Such a big word didn't suit his casual personality. But five drinks can make any man a master philosopher. He spoke from his heart, contrary to the nonchalant image he always presented. I assumed he was finally being true to himself. Dhriti would be lucky to have him in her life; he was eccentric but lovable.

"Do you have nothing else to talk about?" I asked in irritation after a while.

"What else man…this is love. It's non-medicative," he replied, running his fingers through his silky hair.

Not having been successful in turning Aarya's mind from its single focus, I thought it best to escape the 'love express'. Finishing my drink I excused myself for a walk.

I looked at the silvery moon. It shone from the thresholds of clouds, bright and luminous. I could hear the breeze gusting in sulky rhyme. There was something poignant and gripping in that dark sky, heralding another spell of rain. The darkness seemed possessed by a strange premonition. There was something mysterious about the night. The dark glory of the sky, the tantalizing power of the moon, the beauty of the stars flickering in the distance like moments of hope, excited me. The world seemed hidden yet revealed in its true nature. There was something differently romantic and haunting about it. It was the end of the day, the end of hope for some. It was also the precursor of another day of new experiences. For me, I rejoiced in the unknowingness of the night, and what it hid for me. I have always felt darkness tells us something, pushes us forward to know ourselves. I felt under the command of the mysterious night. Perhaps I just needed a long walk to find answers to my questions about balancing action and desire.

I texted Nikhil, asking if he'd like to join me for coffee. His reply was prompt, he was in the canteen. When I got there he was alone, sipping his coffee. I bought myself a cup too, and a packet of biscuits, then went over to where he sat.

"So, not sleepy?" he asked.

"Sort of disturbed; bored more than disturbed actually."

"Disturbed? What's happened?"

"Just not feeling great; had nothing to do; was bored. I decided to take a walk, then changed my mind in favour of coffee, so I texted you in pursuit of fine conversation."

Nikhil gave me a quick, thoughtful glance. "I hope you don't mind if I join you in your pursuit?" His voice was husky, his words a summon rather than a request. My eyes shone.

"What time do you usually sleep?" he asked.

"Late."

"Your voice lacks its normal grace; any health issues?"

"I'm not feeling good."

"It would be rather sad if I failed to brighten up your soul," he said jokingly.

"Ohho! You certainly have the words to soothe the mind."

Under the yellow light I stole a glance at his face. Shadowy trees loomed close to the sidewalk. A cold wind blew. A smile flashed across his face. I could see he was thinking. Our gazes met and merged.

The next moment he pinched my cheeks and exclaimed, "You're a sweet guy!"

I was taken by surprise. I could feel the boil of emotions within me. His face had a compelling charm. "I feel I've known you for ages," I murmured.

He laughed at this. "You sound like a spiritual heretic at times."

I smiled at the remark, stealing another glance at him sipping his coffee.

"This building looks great at night. See the geometric pattern," he said, pointing. "The geometry makes the design."

I took a sip from my own steaming cup. "I don't get geometry," I said.

"I love design. Have you ever visited our ancient Indian temples? They are loud, magnificent and the curves intricate. This is a beautiful building too, the best part being that it is south-east facing, so when the moon shines directly over it, you have great beauty."

"You could have opted for a design course," I suggested.

"The best thing about this particular course is that it allows creativity."

"Which project are you working on?"

"Not working yet, but would like to work on delinquency." I gave him a questioning look. "Juvenile crimes or perhaps war crimes," he explained

"Oh! Not my area of interest. I shall write on travel."

"Well, that's interesting too…"

Back then I never imagined that one day I would become a regular contributor on spirituality and the author of a self-help book, but never have the chance to write on travel.

We finished our coffee and walked into the dark night. The short walk brought me back to life. The laughs we shared, the questions we put to each other, the answerable things in our lives which dropped into the conversation, and the magical spell of the night, brought us closer to each other.

Our walk continued for over two hours as he shared beautiful snippets from his life. He was talkative, a person who had the innate ability to engage you when he chose. We surfed topics ranging from sports to movies to life. Those two hours set the foundation of the beautiful relationship we were to share.

"Good night," he finally said, turning towards his room.

I followed him with my eyes, grateful the night hid the satisfaction on my face. I had taken a step towards my own hostel when I heard him call. I turned back, eyes gleaming.

"You know you should try writing about life, you're very clear about it. Your clarity is as good as my confusion."

Our laughter marked the graceful end of a glorious evening and we parted ways.

Aarya was asleep when I returned. He lay on his bed in his boxers. I looked at him and smiled. I too, fell onto my bed; no thoughts this time.

***

The next day started with a happy thought and a boring class. It was irresistibly difficult not to laugh at Professor Rohatgi's prosaic one-liners, which could have put the great philosophers to shame. It was a talent he had mastered; the other being homicidal assignments. We were in philosophy class, thought to be an elemental trait of the media. Dhriti sat on the next bench; I caught her yawning four times. She must have done the same for me. I knew that after the class I would have two assignments to do, mine and Aarya's.

The Professor spoke about hidden personalities, the blind spot. "At times we go so far into our shells that we lose sight of the things happening around us," he droned.

Someone yawned loudly at the back. "Can it give rise to self-loathing?" I asked.

The class looked at me as if I was a creature from some far planet. Perhaps I was the only one awake.

"At times…yes. At other times it helps you realize your inner self and move from fear to faith," Professor Rohatgi answered.

"But to what extent does it affect the personality of the person?" I saw Dhirti staring at me as the words left my lips.

"It does; it shapes the way you think. It also depends on what particular traits you keep in that shell. It can change the way you think or even the way you act."

"So it is important to open up to someone you trust?"

"Only if you are able to make that out; most people can't," the Professor Rohatgi responded. "But yes, you should always have someone whom you think understands you. Personally I believe one should always be on look for such persons."

"Even when you know the trait you are hiding is wrong?" I asked, ignoring the looks of stupefaction around me.

"First, nothing is 'wrong'. Even the ultimate wrong is right in its own way. And it entirely depends on who defines that wrong. What seems wrong to you may be the ultimate right."

I nodded. Some conversations are short but impactful. I decided to take this discussion further with Professor Rohatgi. There were questions which demanded answers. The Professor resumed teaching but questions kept coming to mind. I parked them for future discussion.

After class, Dhriti came over to me and said, "Boss, you were the only one interested in the class. I couldn't get anything."

"He talks sense; listen to him. You might get answers to your questions," I replied quietly.

"Did you find any?" Aarya asked, sensing a smart chance to start a conversation with Dhriti.

"Hmmm…I will," I smiled. "Excuse me, I'll take my leave." I picked up my bag and left the scene, a blatant attempt to leave them alone.

Aarya and Dhriti looked at each other, surprised by my uncharacteristic behaviour. Aarya must have had an inkling it was part of the plan.

"Isn't he behaving strangely?" Dhriti asked.

Shrugging his shoulders Aarya replied, "I think something has happened. Last night he was off colour but wouldn't tell me why."

"Could be something bothering him…a mental hiccup."

"With him it could be anything really." Aarya gave Dhriti a seductive smile as she stood idly twining the ends of her long silky hair around one finger. "Before the next class starts would you like some coffee?" Aarya asked, heart in mouth.

Somewhat reluctantly, Dhriti agreed. No power on earth could have camouflaged Aarya's delight.

***

Aarya always thanked me for that moment. It was their first coffee together – cappuccino.

"Anu tells me you love music," Dhriti said to Aarya, taking a sip. "What type of music?"

"Soft, subtle, sweet, seductive…" he replied saucily.

She was silent for a moment, then asked, "And what does that mean, *Mr. Aarya?*"

Aarya grinned sheepishly. The unexpected question caught him off guard. Her bright eyes stared straight at him. Something deep within prodded him to be at his best. "Something that brings two souls together," he murmured.

"You craft your words well but I'd like to see your supposedly unique collection."

"Ohh sure…any time ma'am," Aarya said, raising his coffee cup in salute.

"I love good music." Another thoughtful sip and then a golden smile…

The game was on. Smiles say far more than words. I knew Aarya would have difficulty taking the conversation forward so I had texted him to just make her feel relaxed. It seemed to be working.

"I like you guys…you are genuine. Anu keeps telling me about you," Dhriti said.

Aarya grinned, replying smartly, "We can always get to know each other from each other rather through a media."

Dhriti looked at him over the rim of her cup then took another sip. She put the cup down, leaving a line of froth on her upper lip. Aarya's eyes remained riveted to her lips, the smile on his face saying more than any words.

"What's making you smile so much?" she asked.

"Your company."

"And what's so special about my company?"

A casual flirtation was triggering emotions that had the potential of metamorphosing their complacent lives. There was a spark in Aarya's eyes and calmness in her smile. Without saying many words he was lighting up her heart.

"Shall we proceed to class now that break is over?" she asked. A pin called reality burst the balloon of desire. "Be ready with your answer the next time we have coffee," she said, touching him momentarily on the shoulder.

He couldn't help but mutter to himself, 'Girl, you bowl me out!' She had taken just three steps when Aarya called after her, "What if I have my answer ready by this evening?"

"I don't mind having two coffee treats in a day," she giggled as she turned away.

He was left burning with zeal, soft and thick. This small meeting left an imprint on his life – a life he loved. He instantly texted me: *Why do I like her company? She asked me today.*

Because you like her, ass! I texted back.

It has to be something compelling, bro," came the unexpected reply.

Okay, let me think of an answer to please her, I replied.

***

Aarya was excited. I could see it in his face. He narrated the entire story to me in class, a never fading smile on his face. He kept stealing glances at Dhriti. He scribbled something on a piece of paper, twisted it and threw it towards her. She picked it up, read the words and then scribbled something before passing the chit back to him. I kept a straight face though I longed to laugh. Aarya read the note and then passed it to me. He had a puppy dog look on his face.

The note said: 'Coffee at CCD – five?' To which the reply was: 'Aren't you too fast and over-smart?"

Aah! All dreams broken. "Ask her this evening," I advised.

"Will she accept?"

Before I could answer, Professor Das gave us a sharp look.

"Leave him man; tell me, will she accept? How should I approach her?" Aarya whispered, his world now defined by a cup of coffee.

Professor Das took his eyes off the blackboard and caught us chatting. Professors tend to take such things as personal slights. Aarya was turned out of class. I bit back a smile. Dhriti and I exchanged looks, smiles on our faces. I signaled: *For you*. She laughed silently. Such abstractions are like crosswords; reality eludes life for brief moments. Professor Das had his eye on us. We had ignored him at our peril. We too, were turned out of class, only to find Aarya waiting for us.

"I knew the gang was destined to stay together," he said, spreading his arms in warm welcome.

"We all are screwed!" Dhriti announced.

"Then let's go and celebrate. At least he gave us a chance to be together," Aarya suggested.

"You don't seem to need a reason to celebrate, Aarya."

"Life is short Dhriti, and every moment is meant to be celebrated," Aarya answered, calm, composed and in his element. He well knew how to celebrate his life.

We headed to the canteen. Nothing brings two hearts together like venting over food.

"Dar-ji, two *parathas*, one omelette, and Kishoreda songs," Aarya requested before turning back to us. "So what are we going to talk about?"

"Your coffee plans, which got us here in the first place," I said, pulling his leg.

"Look at the positive side; this is our first eat-out together, and that too over good, unhealthy *parathas makhan maar ke,*" Aarya said, unfazed. "I tell you, standing out is fun. Ask me, I have a Masters at that."

Dhriti blushed, her deep smile revealing more than it concealed. She closed her eyes for a minute. Aarya looked at her and smiled too.

It's too hard to run away from love, I thought.

Dar-ji arrived with the orders. "*Lo ji, aloo ka parantha,*"he said in his husky voice as he served us.

The angels of love certainly completed their assignment that day.

*****

5

GAME SET AND MATCH

"That's a nice thing going on," Nikhil commented after I had narrated Aarya's love story on our way to the tennis court.

"June has changed his life," I grinned.

Nikhil stopped. "And when will *your* life change?" he asked, gripping me by the shoulders.

"My life will change when I will defeat you in tennis," I said, forcing a grin to my face.

"Ooohoo! Then your life ends here," he replied, pointing a finger at his racquet.

"No Sir, my life ends here," I replied, pointing at him.

He laughed, but I had said what I had been struggling to say for so long. He held me in his hazel stare for a few seconds, then ordered, "You take the first serve today, and no faults!"

Taking three balls with me, I took my position. Throwing the first ball into the air, I leapt at it like a tiger and hit the shot. *Bang!* On the line. Perfect, I thought.

"More pace Anuj; this won't work," came the critique.

I served again and he returned the shot.

"You must force me to leave the shot alone with a perfect ace. Try for that."

Five serves in a row…he returned them all. I was getting restless, he excited. Learning from him was double fun — friendship and tutelage. We finally settled on a match, a complete set of six games.

"What if I win?" I shouted.

"High tea on me today."

That was too small a prize for such a difficult exercise. I should have asked for a kiss instead. "Fine…even if it's 6-1?" I enquired. The fact was I hadn't won a single game against him. He smiled in agreement.

"So you start this time." I gave him the balls, studying him as he prepared to serve. I was still unsure what I had to study; him or his action. Then the opposite flow started to happen — aces, no returns or loose returns. His shots were bang on.

"I'm gonna play my game. Learn to handle that," he cried at the top of his voice.

I knew there was no chance of winning, or making the score look less shameful. It was David versus Goliath on the court.

"You can do better. Know your opponent, learn his weak areas. You are returning my shots to my right, at a comfortable distance from the body," he instructed.

I was amazed at the quick calculations he could do. I wasn't a bad player but he was the best I had seen, mathematically correct in his shots. He had turned the sport into an art. He said he had found the best opponent on campus in me!

"I couldn't think of any other way of returning that shot," I told him dispiritedly.

"Drop it low or play from a wider angle. In the first case, it will drop near the net, at a good distance from my position. In the latter case, it will drift out of court. Remember how in the previous shot you had pushed me into a corner." He halted. "Don't forget your opponent's position. You are playing well but making the game easy for me."

I nodded and the game went on for more time than usual. It ended at 30:40, a decent score.

"You can take it to deuce. Watch your serve, it needs pace. It should come out like a missile, an out-swinger in cricket."

"I still can't see you losing," I grumbled.

"That means you don't want to see yourself winning."

Now obviously that wasn't the case. We resumed the game. I served, my serve hitting the central line and drifting away from him, well out of his reach. But he sprang on the ball with the agility of a cat and returned the serve, outsmarting me again. I wanted to stride towards him and hug him hard, not out of affection but respect.

"That was a nice serve, a difficult one to return. Even if the opponent manages to do so, he would end up offering an easy opportunity to the server to smash on his left and score. That was a good serve, darting away from the player."

Preparing for the next serve, I tried to take advantage of the wind velocity to make the ball swing away. This strategy, however, played out easily for him. He let the ball come in and with the minimum possible angle from his body, returned the shot; the serve had lost all its pace. I scurried to make up the distance and managed to hit a return, but it was an easy shot for him to smash and score from.

"Remember the rule of opposing forces to maximize your footwork. Push off your left foot to go right. This brings you into a commanding position to play the shot right from body level. Remember, the more the arm is stretched, the more pace the ball gathers. In this situation the best you could have done was to stretch your arm to reach the ball and let your palm twist out so the racquet was at an acute angle to the ball. The ball would have drifted diagonally to my side of the court. You tackled the shot well but failed to read my moves."

I could do nothing but admire the mental gymnastics he was orienting me about. Tennis is not just about the shots – the smash, forehand, backhand, volley and so, but dealing with what your opponent brings to the court. I did manage to win a game that day; perhaps he lost it deliberately to keep my spirits up and the promise alive.

Like good sportsmen we shook hands after the match, our shirts clammy with sweat.

"I need a bath and then we can go out," he said, running a hand over his hair.

"Sure, that sounds great. I'll have a shower, get ready, and come to your room once I'm done," I called, loping off towards my room.

Tea after tennis had become something of a religion with us. Today, as a change, he had suggested adding 'high' to tea. Only he knew what comprised the definition of 'high' – perhaps a finely brewed coffee at Mocha, his caffine indulgence. A coffee lover, he could roll up his sleeves and talk coffee science or get down to brewing it himself. And I always complimented him by repeating the great line: *It takes a great heart and mind to brew an insanely great coffee.*

Having had my shower I got dressed and went over to his room. He was still in his wet t-shirt and shorts from tennis.

"What! Still the same?" I cried, squeezing one arm.

"Sorry…got a call from my mom; give me five minutes." Taking off his shirt he threw it carelessly onto the floor and stood bare-chested. "Your game has improved considerably, you know," he said.

"Hmm…thanks."

He had taken off his shorts and now stood only in his jockeys. I gulped, admiring his butter-coloured skin. I could feel the flush on my face. Tilting my head to one side, I beamed at him. He stood before me, almost naked. I bit my lip, trying not to let my feelings become evident. But my eyes roamed over his body like a glutton at a feast. His ashen nipples and firm butt made me feel dizzy.

"You alright?"

"Oh ye..yes…" I stammered. "You have a soft body."

He looked up with a wicked grin. The next instant he had grabbed my right wrist and twisted my arm behind my back in a tight grip. "So.o.o.f.t?" he asked.

"No…no…I meant virile," I screamed in pain.

He released my arm but grasped me by the shoulders. I lifted my face, smiling with pleasure at being so close to him. I could feel his naked body against mine. His eyes were large and luminous, his lips parted in a smile.

He pulled my cheeks and said, "Don't ever mess with me."

I smiled, wanting to inch forward and indulge in a beautiful kiss. He was so desirable… My eyes trailed over his body, his toned biceps, hairless chest and shaved armpits. I captured him in every detail.

"*Chal*…I'll have a quick shower," he said, releasing me from his delightful grip.

I'm sure I must have had the *oh-please-stay* look in my eyes as he made his way towards the bathroom. I sprawled on his bed and closed my eyes, absorbing every minute of the playful interlude. I stared at the ceiling fan as it spun in my drunken vision. The air around me crackled and I felt myself floating in the clouds of my imagination. I could hear the splashing and felt envious of the water touching his body. Ah! I lived a different life for those few minutes, something I would hold onto forever. Everything was static, yet everything had moved. I closed my eyes, surrendering myself to thoughts of him. I could not contain my jubilation as I made sweet confession to myself.

He emerged with a towel wrapped around his waist, drying his hair with another. "Wake up, sleepy head!" he teased.

"I'm awake," I replied. *How could I miss the visual treat?*

"Can you put some talcum powder on my back?" he asked.

It was the answer to the call of my inner goddess. I gently massaged some talc onto his back. "Your skin *is* soft," I whispered in his ear, my eyes twinkling.

He smiled gleefully and quickly got into his clothes. Picking up the small towel he had used to dry his hair, he put it over my head. I resisted but deep down I enjoyed the way he grasped and played with my hair. He pushed me towards the mirror in the bathroom. The water I had envied lay on the floor; I no longer felt jealous of it, enjoying the child in my romantic hero.

"Can we change our dinner plans?" I asked softly, quiet desperation evident in my eyes.

"Well, we can go to Connaught Place," he suggested.

I nodded dumbly and walked out with him following behind.

***

We took the bus to Connaught Place. I have always admired its environs, which bestow both grandeur and rustiness on Delhi. It is a shopping village as well as a lustful destination for foodies. The signage of the restaurants told simple legends —Mughlai, Chinese, Continental, elegantly dotted with brands like KFC,

CCD and the likes. Connaught Place is like a giant signboard which said: Something For Everyone. I took him to a small, intimate restaurant. It didn't boast any eye-catching signage but the enticing aroma of crisp chicken hung in the air.

"Will this do?" I asked cautiously. He nodded. "It will not burn too big a hole in your pocket," I added, grinning.

The restaurant looked fine to me. Wooden chairs, bright table cloths, decent lighting and walls the same colour as my hostel room – white. The place was chaotic and claustrophobic but irresistible. The air shimmered with tandoor smoke – a paradise for meat lovers, a stop so sinful that I felt like going to confession every time I came here.

"The *shawarma is* worth trying here," I suggested.

"You are entrusted with the responsibility of making this dinner memorable for me. Order whatever you would like me to try," he responded, cool and collected.

"That would prove too heavy for your wallet to bear," I laughed. Seeing him getting defensive I added with a saleman's smile on my face, "But we can go Dutch. The bold idea is to not let our gastronomic buds know when to stop."

"I always thought you were a veggie…at least you look like one," Nikhil said, leaning back in his seat.

"I am mostly, but I can also devour anything. You love lemon chicken I know, and the command is to get dishes you love. So should we go with that. And dessert is on me as a treat for teaching me tennis. I know a great place for that," I added with feeling.

"Had I known I would be treated for teaching you tennis, I'd have done so from the day you entered college," he chortled as the waiter served us water.

"I expected you to say, 'I would have waited for you, with racquet in hand, at the college gates,'" I said, mimicking him.

The waiter brought us menu card and after a little discussion we ordered five dishes. "Enough to fill the table *and* our stomachs," I commented happily.

"*Yupp*! Gluttony is one sin everyone should commit," he joked lightly, a sweet line curving from his mouth to his eyes. "This seems a good place," he murmured.

"I wouldn't have brought you here otherwise. In fact, this is one of the best places I've found in Delhi. The service is quick."

"I'm glad we came. It's been ages since I went for an eat-out," he sighed.

"You seem quite the party guy to me. You know, when I first saw you, you were the soul of the party…"

Before I could complete my observations he said, "But I'm not. I am friend to a few. You'll rarely find me talking intently or intimately with anyone."

He smiled. I smiled back.

"Then I should thank the guy sitting up there," I said, pointing skywards. "So what did you find so extraordinary in me that you not only get into intense and intimate conversations with me but also come out to dinner with me?"

"*Hahaha…*" he laughed. "I never said you're the only one but yes, something keeps you in a special category in my life."

We kept asking each other pointless questions, narrating stories about our childhood, before diving into serious discussions about careers and life. We lost track of time till the waiter brought us our food. Then we busied ourselves eating, telling futile stories, laughing over things that weren't very funny, arguing about issues that didn't matter and sharing smiles as we ate. He relished the food, I could see. I enjoyed his company and getting to know the different shades of his life. He seemed to make a point of not wasting food. He ate like there were no tomorrow.

"It's so satisfying to watch you eat," I remarked.

He laughed ruefully. "This is so good! I should have come here before."

"I'm happy to know you love it. I've been planning on coming here for a long time," I replied, pouring some more gravy onto his plate.

"We could have more eat-outs; this isn't too expensive."

"Never fear, I'll take you to the secret lanes of Delhi, where food is as diverse as it is yummy," I promised recklessly.

"I would love to join you on such an exploration – a date with the culinary culture of Delhi!"

"I would love going-on-a-*date*-with-you," I said, clipping off each word and stressing *date* to get his attention. I poured us some water, the ice cubes clinking in our glasses.

He laughed. "You love dating guys?"

"Yeah…" I waited for his eyes to meet mine before adding, "But only if the guy is as irresistible as you."

I smiled. He smiled. Life has a way of making up for past desires and hopes. My desires were evident in my eyes; they could not lie.

We decided to take a walk after dinner. The razzmatazz of the shopping dens of Delhi seems mystical to me. One can so easily be dazzled by the brightness of Delhi's markets. We decided to go a little further. Just two streets away, haggle-free handicrafts stood and hung in an entrancing jumble.

"This happens to be my favourite place," I said. "The word 'selection' has to be taken very seriously here," I said, pointing towards the heart-melting handicrafts and handlooms.

"You love these things?"

"Look at the intricacy, the detail in the workmanship, the fine craftsmanship," I enthused. "One day, when I am earning, I will have these treasures in my living room. It's a beautiful place. When you have gifts to buy, come here."

"I shall ask you to bring me."

His hands brushed against mine and my eyes lit with delight.

"And yes, irresistible one, I will."

My laughter mixed with his. For a moment there was just us, hands touching, hearts beating.

"Then I'll wait for our second date," he said humorously.

"So, have you ever dated before?"

"If I say no?"

"*Uhmm*…then I'd say I am even luckier than I thought I am." I joked and he gave me a half hug.

We took the metro and headed back to college. Those moments with him left an indelible mark on my life. For a time I forgot my vulnerability. Somewhere deep in my heart there was optimism, a feeling that this time I would not be left struggling to find my identity, wrestling with my demons. I was happy. I had an arm across his shoulders as we talked at length about his likes and dislikes. Some moments can make you feel alive; I know their value. They are rare and ephemeral, dying before one can live them fully. Yet this time I vowed to live each moment, putting aside any thoughts of loss.

***

It took me just a few days to fall for Harshit. His intense smile arrested me, drawing me closer every time I saw him. I did not realize how quickly I started noticing everything about him — the way he smiled or threw back his head when he laughed, or the way his eyes lit up when saying 'hello'. His eyes seemed vulnerable; serious with a concentrated, constant gaze. That was in class 11 and love hormones were on a high. The small but inciting daily interactions with him made me feel I had grown wings, ready to soar high. I never realized how soon my whole life became condensed to one face, the smile that always had me surrendering to it. A little mole next to his lips added to its beauty. I was in a trance, a moth drawn to a flame — slowly but irreversibly, with absolute intensity. I felt myself disintegrating into a million pieces but they always merged with him. I had fallen in love.

He had a subtle commanding charm to his voice. For the first few days, I was indecisive, to love him or not… He never noticed my quaint feelings.

I squinted, stealing glances at him. While my heart thudded each time his hands accidently brushed against mine, he remained indifferent to my looks and my feelings.

I started staying late to watch him play soccer, smiling at the lack of welcome in his life. He seemed unreachable to me. Yet his exuberance on scoring a goal never failed to touch me. Every casual smile I received in return for my hand raised in congratulation worked like poetry on my soul. I watched him with the curiosity of a new mother. I searched him with the eyes of naked love — the slope of his shoulders, the tips of his fingernails, the arches of his thighs, taut with regular exercise. I searched for him in my dreams and in the stories I narrated to myself every night. I longed to watch his athletic gait.

I laughed thinking of our irreconcilable apartness. I failed to make a move; he failed to understand that I came to watch him and not the game. With every smile I retreated into stillness. The fear of consequences killed every smile, like an unwilling whisper, a bud destined to die before blooming. How can a man love a man? I couldn't go to him and say: 'I love you…I dream of you, I take you to my bed every night without any thought of absolution for my sin.' I couldn't. I wouldn't. I shouldn't.

*****

6

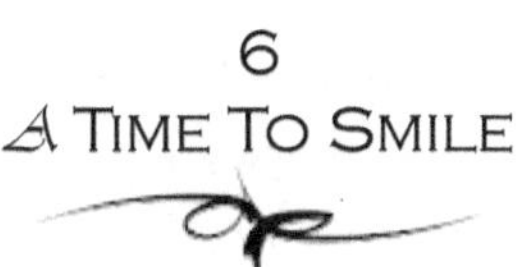 A TIME TO SMILE

"Hey man, it's been a great day! I dined with Dhriti and we had a long chat," Aarya announced in a victorious voice.

I took off my shoes. "Now that's news! Details please…" I responded, eager for more.

"Man, you can't imagine how eagerly I've been waiting for you to return…to tell you the whole story." He seemed ready to explode with happiness.

I forced a laugh. "Cool…you got your girl."

"So where have you been?" I suddenly realized I had not told him about my dinner date.

"I defeated Nikhil in a game of tennis today, so he treated me to dinner, in celebration. We went to a small restaurant and ate chicken like cats that had not been fed for a week," I said, condensing my date story while rolling my eyes and taking up a comfortable position.

"So I asked her out to dinner. She sort of resisted at first but then agreed. We went to a Chinese restaurant and tried some new dishes I've never heard of before in Gwalior," he confessed, smiling. "She chose, she ordered, and I paid the bill," he told me ecstatically.

"But did you tell her about your feelings for her?"

"Not explicitly, but she's intelligent enough to know."

"That she is but you will still have to be explicit. Girls like to be made to feel special. You'll have to do that for her – make her feel she's the lucky one."

Outside the sky curdled and the clouds resolved themselves into little lumps. The moon shone between them, struggling to keep its shine.

Aarya looked at me. "I feel this date was too normal," he said, wondering if it was wise to call it a date.

"There's always another chance to make it better," I remarked.

His face lit up. "So what should my next move should be?"

"Message her right now, thanking her for her company. Then keep a watch to catch any signals. See, if the girl seems happy in your company or is constantly stealing glances, or smiling at your silly jokes, or keeps twirling a strand of hair as she listens to you, or looks at you shyly, then brother, the ball is rolling for you. Now tell me, did she seem comfortable?"

I was full with answers. He stared at me, a broad smile on his face. Gleaming brown eyes bored into mine.

***

An after-dinner constitutional had become a regular practice with me, driven by sexual churnings. I had always loved the night. I enjoyed drenching myself in its mystery. There was a distinctive smell of rain in the air and the dead leaves swirled in restless wind. The moon occasionally appeared through the cloud cover, and a world of shadows cloaked me in anonymity. The darkness of the night hid much for me.

For days now things had been progressing in the desired direction. Nikhil now felt at ease with me, spent time with me and even borrowed some of my things. He teased, jibed and consoled. In just a few days we had grown deeply fond of each other. I sensed this fondness wasn't like the one I shared with Aarya. There was something highly contagious about it. I knew I was slipping out of control… But what of Nikhil, I wondered as I headed for our usual coffee rendezvous.

"For a change I've got toast and butter for us," he announced.

I sat down beside him. He did not seem to mind the closing distance between us. The intense momentum of our growing closeness would have left physicists baffled. A few weeks ago we barely knew each other. He became aware of my existence in the small world of the tennis court. Soon polite smiles metamorphosed into genuine acknowledgements, to short talks. Time flew by as we bared our hearts and souls to each other, bit by bit. We both knew this fondness was different.

Nikhil was an adorable pest who adapted quickly in unknown waters. We were from different batches but helped each other with assignments and soon constructed our own little world of gossip. He danced into my life with such ease, making me believe I was incomplete without him. My eyes looked for him in every corner; my inbox was full of his messages. I even shouted his name from my balcony once.

Over every cup of coffee we shared, I yearned for a kiss. I was deep in love and it was visible in all my actions. I hugged him often, pulled his hair, texted him before exams. I cared. I kept getting deeper into the game, sans guilt, sans logic, sans fear of consequences. I never even attempted to restrain myself.

The sky was laced with a little moonshine. The wind still carried a monsoon chill, promising quiet, quilted romance.

"I enjoy your company…" I murmured quietly; words so inadequate to the need of the hour!

"And I hate it when you state the obvious," he retorted.

I then did something that was *not* obvious. It took but a second of madness. I put a hand on his thigh, an arm around his shoulder and kissed him…on the lips. It was impromptu, without any thought. His smile vanished. I tried putting on a synthetic smile but could not hold onto it. His face was pale. We were both shocked by what had just happened.

He lowered his gaze and whispered, "It's not the right place for… for a return kiss."

It took me a minute to absorb what he had said. My eyes twinkled and I pinched myself to make sure I wasn't dreaming. The words resonated in my ears. "*Wooo…hooo…*" I cried aloud, my voice silencing the songs of the night. I caught him in my arms and hid my face in his hair.

"I said this is not the right place," he said again.

Somewhere deep in my belly I could feel the fire. We walked silently towards the garden, isolated in inky darkness, infamous for snakes. The right place…

"So you?" I murmured.

"Don't know really…but I could feel you liked me. You wouldn't have tried coming so close otherwise."

I smiled, my eyes failing to meet his. If only he knew how much I'd tried to get close! "Why didn't *you* start this?" I asked softly.

"I was afraid…and confident you'd open up some day."

"You were the doyen of my wet dreams," I told him.

He gave a brief laugh, coming close. "Now just shut-up! I have to return something."

Nikhil brought his mouth down on mine, hard. We were caught in the sweet act, the night unclothing our tantalizing desires. Seconds passed and then a minute. He kissed intensely. He unlocked my senses with a sinful smile. His drunken eyes played tricks with me. It was my first kiss, probably his, too. The floodgates of carnal desire burst open.

"Nikhil, it's late…perhaps we should make a move."

"Are you sure you want to go?" he asked, his voice raspy with lust.

"I won't be able to hold myself much longer."

"Okay…but I loved it."

"Me too…"

I turned and hastily made my way towards the hostel. On the way I texted: *I love you*. I wanted to say more but didn't have the nerve. I was literally unable to contain myself and quickly ducked behind some bushes. Glancing around to make sure I was alone, I slid my jeans and briefs to the ground. Drops of pre cum oozed from my tender, virgin penis head. I grabbed my shaft frantically. It didn't take long for my lust to wash over the leaves, mute witnesses to my ecstacy. I felt unbelievably good; I experienced a sense of liberation, of accepting my devils as gods. Remembering that kiss I knew I would sleep in bliss tonight.

My phone buzzed. The message read: *Love you too. Good night.*

***

Certain moments take you back in life.

He playfully rubbed my thighs. An involuntary, disbelieving giggle escaped me. I bit my lips, awed by the sensation. A hundred images of my inner goddess, dancing and jiving with joy, passed through my mind, each in Harshit's glorious wrap. I wanted to do the same to him; maybe he expected that. Our glances met. Something that had taken so many days was happening. He smiled, his eyes lit with frolic, mine with desire. It seemed the moment to vent my feelings. My hands involuntarily rubbed his thighs. At first my brain failed to register what I saw, but strong tremors had begun to race through my spine. I was transfixed; I was getting what I had been asking for. I was reeling with pleasure. Neither of us had ever mentioned it, but my eyes inadvertently expressed my feelings and he knew. Ah! I wished I could hold that moment for perpetuity. I knew it would be over once all the lab instructions were given and we had taken our seats. Shivering, I dropped my pen as something rose in me, seeking release. All my energy seemed to accumulate at a single point in my body. It controlled me. I felt like a thousand waves were crashing over me. I wanted to scream but all I could do was gasp. The unreachable was so close. I peeked at the others in class, just to reassure myself that no one had caught us in this compromising situation.

I couldn't offer the slightest resistance to the hand that cheekily inched towards my groin. It was a mute romance. I was dazzled by his powers. With trembling fingers I carefully followed the path he led me on, following his actions, pleasing him the way he was pleasing me. My powers of volition were completely paralyzed. Something egged me on, all I wanted was to close my eyes and feel him. The intensity and smoothness with which he touched my body made my limbs turn soft and languid, all my blood rushing to the love centre. My imagination briefly traversed a different path — my body under his control, skin to skin, together.

My forehead glistened with cold sweat. Passion had taken control of my body and mind. Everything around me seemed unreal, unpalpable. For a moment my senses stopped working as he firmly clasped my hand and put it on his thigh. I bit my lip and stole a glance at him; his smile was different, one of possession. My eyes looked down, possessed, desiring, intimate. He shook his head, his attention on my fingers. My heart constricted. His smile made me feel strong, loved, desired. Deliberately, I bit my lip and shook my head.

The next minute we were called for our practical — the dissection of a cockroach to study its muscle fibres. Urgh! After such a sublime sensation, it seemed the cruellest thing possible. All interest in biology died. I delivered a sharp blow to the dead cockroach and with the forceps, removed its limbs. The boy next to me asked annoyingly, 'How to do this?' Infuriated, I replied, 'This way!' and dissected the other limb of the poor creature. I could sense the impulse still within me and stole a glance. He was holding his cockroach with forceps like a trophy.

I dragged myself along the school corridor, lost in thought, his triumphant smile flashing before my eyes. I could see the pariah kites soaring high in the sky, drawing energy from that imperishable source, imbibing the dazzling sunlight to fire up the bio-chemics in the body to metabolise the photons into energy. But I felt enfeebled by that warmth; heated and wearied, somehow consumed by that brilliant light. My thoughts flickered like a candle flame, dancing in the over-warm breeze. A mirage grew before me and I moved closer, anticipating an oasis of love. It was insidious and baffling! His smile flashed before my eyes again. He seemed everywhere — in my thoughts, in my prayers, in my game. I couldn't keep my mind off him. For the first time someone had touched me deeply. I had felt his fingers take control of my mind, something rising in me. It was a lovely feeling. Scattered thoughts of him kept crossing my mind. I had tasted desire and I loved it.

I traced my steps towards the bathroom and banged the door shut. I masturbated calling his name, to feel complete — for the first time in my life. I bit my lip, wishing I could tell him. I laughed out loud. The freaky kite had found the sun and was sinking into its dazzling light. I imagined him holding me, his lips soft on my shoulder, his nose against my ear.

***

"She said yesss!" Aarya whispered to me in class. He had deliberately dragged me to the last bench so he could tell me.

"Who…Dhriti?" I asked, pretending ignorance.

"Who else?" he replied blissfully.

"Well that was pretty fast; just a fortnight!" I said in a single breath. "So what's next?"

"You should go for longer walks now," he suggested.

I was aghast. "You wanna invite her to our room? What if the hostel security sees?"

He chuckled. "See who's getting rattled now! Anyway, there's a long way to go before that. Love is a game of understanding," he added wisely.

Things had changed dramatically in an instant, turning him into a love sage. The thought brought a smile to my face. He kept talking and I listened, not uttering a single word.

"Are you even listening?" he whispered urgently. I nodded. "Anyway, you'll have to help me take this forward to a never-ending relationship."

We had caught the attention of Professor Das. Result: another stand-outside-the-class session; they had become as frequent as power cuts.

"Cool, we've been thrown out of class!" Aarya said nonchalantly. "I wanted to talk about something important,"

"You did that deliberately to catch Prof's attention?"

"You weren't listening. There was no other option," he explained.

"We could have talked after class." I moved towards the canteen. The desperate lover followed.

"So...." he started to explain again. "You know you are my best friend..." He waited for me to nod, a master of flattery. "Anyway, I know you're angry for getting us kicked out of class, and you have every right to be, but you know I am deeply in love. I have no repose. There is no coming back from where I have gone. And now, when things are looking good, I wanna make them great!" He waited for my reaction and I for coffee.

After a scalding, soothing sip, I murmured, "You told me she had agreed."

"To friendship. I haven't told her the big thing yet."

"Don't worry, she must have understood that by now; her inner goddess must be jumping like a cheerleader with pom-poms," I joked.

"I hope so," he replied, flushing. Aarya scanned the canteen then stared at me, his face impassive and inscrutable.

I could feel his longing; I knew well how it felt. "It'll just be some days," I said in a calm, measured tone, breaking the brief silence between us.

He nodded in acceptance. I wondered why any girl would ever say no to him. Being in love was, as Aarya was wont to say, un-medicative. A single smile at the breakfast table tells you that someone has missed you; a gentle touch sets your day rolling with thoughts of that someone. Yeah, life can never be more beautiful or you more helpless than when you are in love. Your eyes try to find someone in the crowd and you yearn to see the person wave to you. Sweet, simple emotions become the only language you understand. I found myself hypnotized by Nikhil's gaze, felt my belly muscles clench as the shadow of a smile caressed his lips. I inhaled deeply when he touched me. I felt the surge in my body when he kissed me. My heart raced every time I felt his eyes on me. I knew I loved and lusted after him. I lived him.

I wished I could share my story with Aarya, but he would not have understood. But I had never needed his acceptance. Harshit's face crossed my mind. I hadn't been wrong then either. I had just loved him.

***

Nikhil asked me to come to the library. It felt good to know he wanted to be with me as much as I wanted to be with him. He was sitting in a corner, reading.

"Hey!" I interrupted. He looked up and smiled. "What are you reading?" I asked.

"Nothing much…a magazine for time-pass," he replied, putting down the publication on the table. He looked at me. I enjoyed having all his attention. He was a master of the art of seduction.

"So what's so urgent that you called me here right after class?" I asked, trying to sound stern.

"I wanted to ask you about the other night," he said quietly, looking around to ensure we were alone.

I blushed. "It was my first," I revealed.

"For me, just the second."

"You never told me…" I said, surprised.

"Hmm…it was just a kiss after a movie," he shrugged.

"Must have been one hot movie," I joked.

"Just experimental…it was just a kiss, nothing more."

"Who initiated it?"

"I did. It was great! We kissed for a while, then everything evaporated."

"This time it won't," I promised. We had found our mates.

"I'd like to ensure that. Let's go to the bathroom; there's no one around," he suggested.

I smiled. There was no one but us in the library, with no possibility of interruption. I followed him to the bathroom and he bolted the door.

"Are you mad?" I whispered. "What if someone comes?"

"You should have thought of that before entering," he said, holding me by the waist and pushing me against the wall. My sub-conscious seemed to emigrate. I felt dumbstruck, able to absorb but unable to articulate my feelings. I could hear the rustle of his old, faded, ripped jeans as he stepped closer to me. He opened the basin tap and flicked some drops of water onto my face. I closed my eyes.

"What happened?" he asked.

"I'm nervous…what if someone sees?"

"Two boys can go into a bathroom together, right? A boy and a girl cannot," he answered, smiling impishly

"Yeah, but if someone sees two guys in a compromising situation, it makes news."

"You will be in a wilful situation, not compromising," he said, running a finger along my hairline.

My heart was thudding with fear and nervousness. I could feel his breathing, the enticing charm of his hazel eyes compelling me to willingly surrender myself.

"I want to love you," came the soft whisper, his breath smelling of mint. Cocking his head to one side, he inched closer till there was no gap left between us. He put his lips on mine. The next instant our tongues rolled over each other. I moaned with pleasure as he slid his hands under my t-shirt, holding my waist. He pressed his lips against my neck. Every kiss seemed to reflect my deep-seated emotions and vulnerabilities. My dirty goddess, a mute spectator to my fears, broke free. My lips moved while my hands trembled, contradicting each other, betraying different emotions. His passion intruded on me. Instead of holding him guilty, I felt beguiled by the romantic poetry of his kisses.

"Sorry, but I couldn't wait for the night," he said apologetically.

"Hmm…" I moaned, my eyes evading his.

Grasping my chin, he forced my eyes to meet his. "You okay?" he asked tenderly, a finger caressing my lips.

I nodded, making an honest attempt not to offend him. I could feel my belly muscles clenching with pleasure. He put his right palm on my cheek while his left hand traced my lips. "If you don't want this, we can wait," he said, his voice strained.

My eyes met his. My breathing accelerated. I leaned forward and kissed him softly. His hand moved from the side of my cheek to hold the side of my head. I wanted to run my fingers through his hair but I resisted. Our kiss gradually grew intense as I surrendered myself to him. "Nik…." I cried, drowning in desire.

He rubbed his hands over my back, wrapping them around me like silk. Our heartbeats raced and our souls burned with desire. My eyes met his — that deep, intense, promising gaze that never failed to drive me mad, the long lashes, the salacious grin on wet lips smeared with the colours of my love and liberation, the slow smile searching for clues in my eyes. I was nervous and excited, living moments I had constructed in my imagination since I first saw him. I had longed for this closeness since I realized I loved Harshit.

"I love you," I said.

"Me too…" he smiled.

I took refuge in his warm embrace.

"Should we go?" he whispered.

"I want to hold onto this moment Nik. I feel exultant."

"I know…you were lonely. You wanted to open up. I could feel that in you."

"Why didn't I ever feel that about you?" I asked curiously.

"You did, otherwise you wouldn't have kissed me that day," he replied.

The episode flashed before my eyes. I wondered if that had been confidence or desperation. He trailed a finger down my cheek to my chin, on down my neck to the hollow in my throat. I gulped, gasping for breath, covered in sweat, feeling the shock of an orgasm denied. I felt disoriented.

"You make me feel so happy, Nik…"

"I'm glad I do that," he chuckled. "*Chale?*"

I wanted to stay there in his arms, feeling him, living him. He went out, telling me to follow in a few minutes. I took a deep breath, leaning against the basin. Moments passed like a dream, leaving me floating in my sub-conscious. I splashed water on my face in an attempt to get back to reality. I panted, yearning to explode.

He was calmly sitting in the library, turning the pages of a magazine. He greeted me with a comforting smile, acting like nothing had happened. The entire episode seemed to have left him untouched.

"You are sweating."

"I'm just a bit nervous," I answered in a subdued voice. "I feel good when you are around, but then I don't know…I feel nervous too," I stammered.

"Anu, ask yourself if you want this relationship."

"Sure I do." I was quick to respond.

"Then don't worry."

***

The sky seemed painted in random shades. There was a sullen dryness in the wind. I have always had a great affection for the setting sun. It places before you nature's beautiful art collection.

I was making my way home. I knew the two ladies of my house would be eagerly waiting to see me and a series of questions would follow; odd comments would be made about my health, the lost sheen of my adorable face and my tense look. The irony is that only a mother can tell how much brightness has waned from your face, no machine or mirror can. And before you can explain, they come up with a super recipe for all ills — *maa ki haath ki roti*. Such moments imprint themselves on your heart. Like most Indian guys my age, I loved my mother, yet failed to acknowledge the concern she had for me.

I rang the door bell. The other lady of the house opened it. She screamed, I screamed, as we siblings greeted each other.

"Hey bro, how are you?" A predictable question.

"Cool Di, I'm good." A predictable answer.

"After so many days, busy bee."

Aah! The first taunt! "I get free from dumb classes only in the evening." *Out came the answer I had parroted for so long.*

"Boy, I wasn't born yesterday…"

I was left speechless but soon recovered. "Di, I visited just a few days ago." The sharp look I got caused me to amend my claim. "Ohkay…few weeks, maybe a month." *I auto-corrected to avoid further words of combat.*

"You better have a better answer for Mom." *The greatest irony is you can fool anyone in the world except your mom.*

I winked and asked, "Where is she?"

"With the lover she couldn't marry — Lord Krishna."

Her humour has certainly improved. "How's your work going?" I asked, changing the topic.

"Being in a Government Public Affairs department you realize there is no difference between good and bad." *I should have known better than to ask. Talk about work and she blows a fuse.*

"That's an old story. Get me some tea." *She made a face at the idea of action; she was a government employee after all.*

Even though we are like two banks of a river, we constantly refer to ourselves as 'we'. She was my first friend and confidanté. She gave me financial aid when I needed money and was my emotional guide when I felt low. She convinced my father to let me take up mass media studies although he always had a four-word answer to all questions regarding my career: *Engineer dad, engineer son.* He almost sang it like an anthem.

I had only taken the first sip of my tea when the first lady of the house arrived, done with her date with God. She waved the *puja thali* before me then offered me a sweet as *prasad.*

"Now, tell me how you are," she said, following this with a predictable series of questions.

"I'm happy to see you like college life," Di commented. "I can see some change in you."

"Change…what sort of change?" I asked, a quizzical look on my face.

"You seem lively…it seems you are *living* life. I always sensed some sort of fear in you before. It has vanished now," she said, taking me into her arms for deep comfort.

"How can you guess so much?"

"My donku, I don't need you to tell me to know that."

"But, if you knew there was something wrong in my life, why didn't you ever ask me?" I had the same quizzical expression on my nonplussed face.

"Because I knew you would tell me one day," she said, sighing deeply. "Let *me* tell you one thing – life throws a lot of questions at us, but none are so difficult that they are left unanswered."

I could hear the concern in her voice and smiled, trying to hide the pain in my eyes. I could have opened up to her that day; I knew she would have stood by me, but I waited.

"Anuj, start loving yourself, it's the best thing you can do. If being in college gives you a reason to smile, for whatever reason, don't miss that opportunity."

"You know what Di, you should quit your job and get into counselling and healing, and whatever spirituality you have learnt and practiced."

My words fell on her like gentle rain. I saw a smile spread across her face.

"The time for that isn't yet," she said quietly.

A comforting silence followed this brief conversation, broken by my mother calling us for dinner. I looked at Di, realizing I wouldn't be able to hide the truth from her much longer.

*****

7

Aarya's Big Day

"Aarya!" someone yelled, knocking feverishly at the window.

The opague image of Dhriti appeared. She called again, asking him to open the back door for her.

Aarya's face glowed with excitement as he rose to let her in. "If anybody sees, we'll both be rusticated," he said, pulling her into the room and banging the door shut.

"Oooh…that was close!" Dhriti exclaimed. "Now it's okay… whatever happens in this room remains in this room, and not goes before the hostel discipline squad. Where's Anu?"

"He has gone home on a visit…why?"

"Because I have work with him."

"Well, he's not here but I can be put to good use," he offered. "It's good you came because I was about to call you."

"Oh! Call me…for?"

"I was getting bored, so I thought we could go for a walk." He broke down each word, his eyes spinning a charm so that the words sounded like a holy incantation of love.

She smiled but chose to change the topic. "It was dangerous coming to the boy's hostel. I had to hide from so many eyes, but it was adventurous too," she said defiantly. "Anyway, what were you doing?" she asked, planting herself on Aarya's bed.

It was good she couldn't see the stashed treasure trove of whiskey bottles and cigarettes, which would have shocked her innocent soul. Fortunately I had cleaned that before I left.

"You are giving all the wrong signals here – a boy, a girl, a dark room…both eager to get spoilt," he said, attempting to induce humour into the situation as he took a step towards her.

"Do you mind keeping your distance, mister?" she hissed.

He always knew how not to let an opportunity go to waste. He narrowed the distance between them. He could see acceptance in her eyes before she punched him lightly and threw the pillow at him. He caught it, tossed it aside and moved forward to get hold of her. "Baby…let's get spoilt," he said playfully.

"You jerk!" she cried, punching him in an attempt to free herself.

"Oh I love that…" he cried, holding her by her shoulders.

She pushed him, but this time he took her along for the fall. She was right over him, in a locked dark room, girl over boy. That would have made news on campus. They began to laugh hysterically, his hands on her waist, hers on his chest. Her breath mixed with his as she looked deep into his eyes. A feeling of comfort lay in their depths.

"Aar…ya…" she stammered, trying to say something.

"Sshhh…" He was enjoying the silence between them, ready to explode into a volcano of love. "You came to meet me didn't you?" he whispered into her ear.

She smiled. She had come to meet him. His face inched forward and his nose rubbed against hers. He saw her close her eyes, her warm breath on his face. Her lips were dangerously close to his, waiting to be kissed. He felt the movement of her cheek as she readied herself for the kiss and knew the time was right. He inched forward and his lips touched hers. She didn't retract. The kiss continued, dragging him into oblivion. His hand moved over her back into her hair. Her pounding heartbeat resonated in his head. It was more beautiful than the most romantic embrace he had ever imagined, with both of them smiling between each perfect kiss. They cuddled up to each other, she resting her head on his chest.

"Is that it?" he asked playfully.

Her smile said: *No pranks*. She said, "I think I should get down."

"Thanks, you're heavy!"

"Shut up!" She gently slapped his cheek.

Smiling, he gripped her hand and shoved it away. Laughing, she continued to playfully slap him.

"Now tell me why you came here?" he murmured, his hands gently caressing her cheeks.

She listened intently, kissed his fingers and answered, "Because it's fun coming to the boy's hostel; taking all those risks to meet your boyfriend."

"Going to the girl's hostel; taking all the risks involved to meet one's girlfriend, would be equally fun," he replied cheekily.

"Ah, but then my room-mate is not a local and doesn't take every Saturday off…so there's a twist in the story," she replied, running her hands through his silky hair.

"I love you!" he breathed, planting a soft kiss on her parted lips.

She smiled and whispered, "I know you love me, and it's time you should know I love you too." She dexterously undid the top two buttons of his shirt and kissed his chest. She felt aroused by his raw sexuality and her own bubbling feelings.

He turned towards her, placing his right leg between hers. He toyed with the silky hair brushing against his face. "You look beautiful!" How he had longed to tell her that! He inched forward to kiss her again. Their lips met and locked.

***

I had not yet reached college when I received a message from Aarya about his first kiss. I laughed, happy for them. I messaged Nikhil to meet me at the canteen. *Come to my room; I'm alone*, was the quick reply. In another few minutes I was there, something holding me rooted there.

He pulled me in and bolted the door. "So how is everyone at home?" he asked.

"Fine," I answered solemnly.

"You sound tired," he said, sensuously touching my cheek. I submissively accepted.

He offered me some biscuits, saying in a concerned voice, "You should take care of yourself." He moved forward to kiss me but I quickly moved away before he could so and planted myself on his bed.

"I feel guilty," I cried.

"Guilty…about our relationship? Are you feeling guilty about who you are or of what you are doing?"

"About who I am. What will I tell my parents?"

He sat down beside me. "You cannot keep feeling guilty all your life. Deep down, I know I'm gay. I don't tell people about it, but when I see guys around me, my heart makes my mind realize who I am and I duly accept my reality." He took a deep breath. "When I kiss you I feel my existence in you. For society, we are different; for us, society is indifferent,"

I nodded my head in agreement. "You're still a kid, you know," he said, a hand on my hair.

I looked up at him and smiled. "And you aren't my father," I replied in a low tone.

"I'm just your lover. And lovers are supposed to take care of each other."

"I fell in love with you the day I saw you," I admitted.

"I know; you were very predictable." He offered me some biscuits. "So tell me – if I'm not wrong, you are bottom?"

I looked at him, completely puzzled. "I'm what?"

He grinned, placing a hand on my thigh. "Kiddu, in bed with another guy, do you like to be on top or bottom?"

"Will we have sex?" I asked in a feeble tone, feeling butterflies in my stomach.

"Don't tell me you've never had the dreams I have," he said, seductively rubbing my thigh.

His touch produced a tantalizing effect. Dreams…I had imagined him in broad daylight.

"You didn't reply to my question," he said, sitting still.

Silence percolated between us.

"I want you over me, complementing ourselves, freeing ourselves from our fears," I murmured.

"Ah! The black man needs the white man to free him from his fears; the white man needs the black man to free him from his guilt," Nikhil remarked, smiling.

"What?"

Nikhil was taken aback by the sharpness in my voice and said simply, "They are not my words, just paraphrased from Martin Luther."

"I get that there is a conflict of needs." A thought blitzed through me. "I know what I need, but I still don't know what you need. But I will find out soon enough."

"In life you just have to press the right buttons for the right answers," he said, uncurling my palm to kiss it.

"There are nevertheless some questions left unanswered," I insisted, trying to subtly inch away.

"I'll delete those questions from your life," he promised, leaning towards me.

"You didn't tell me about your first kiss," I said.

He laughed. "You're very eager to know about me. I know you too, have a story deep within. Am I allowed to know it?"

"Mine is a sad story; just leave it." I suddenly remembered Harshit; he had been virtually deleted from my memory over time.

"You fell for a straight guy who didn't accept you," Nikhil announced.

I smiled, my smile telling all.

"It happens. Mine happened with a friend, after watching a movie. He agreed. We kept our need-based relationship going for quite a few days, in fact months. It was not a relationship really, just seeking sexual benefits. Then he backed out. But that quick fling taught me that I like guys. In our case your feelings were obvious and I developed an inclination towards you. You stalked me, followed me to the swimming pool, tried to turn every chance meeting into an opportunity for conversation. It was all visible in your eyes, my dear."

"You knew all that?" I asked, blushing like a girl.

"That proved to be a good thing for me, for you wouldn't have opened up...*ever*."

"By the way, in the interest of exactitude, it was I who kissed you first," I said, inching towards him. "I may tie you up some day," I muttered crabbily.

"For that you'd have to catch me first," he said, springing up from the bed and leaving me lying flat on my back.

His words brought back how I had chased him around college, finding a suitable corner, the thrill…and the aftermath. I frowned, shuddering at the unnerving thought. Seeing my lack of interest in the chasing game, he came back to sit on the bed, his brows drawn together, thinking, *Nerd boyfriend!* He sat in the circle of my arms in comfortable, companionable silence.

***

Aarya hugged me the instant I entered the room. "Hey it's done!" he cried in excitement. "Let's have a party!"

He didn't give me time to decipher the reason for the party so I made a guess. "So…she couldn't remain immune to your looks?" I suggested as he made me a drink.

"You were right. It was good. I gave time for things to happen on their own."

"Gave time?" I sounded like a scalded cat. "Brother, it happened like lightening! You were quick to hit the target."

"You seem to know a lot about all this. But you've never told me your story," he said musingly.

"There's no story worth the telling. I never felt the need of a story to define me. I'm just happy as I am."

"*Need* sounds innocuous but it's a powerful word, brother."

"Yeah…it is. The instant we stop needing, we transcend everything. But in this case, you can believe me."

"Okay, leave all this philosophy; that's your domain. I need to tell you about my first kiss," he said happily.

"Oh sure," I replied, not the least bit interested.

He began the tale, with every minute highlighted as an episode of the love saga. There was exuberance in his voice. I remembered Nikhil's words, 'Your clarity is as good as my confusion' and smiled.

***

Thoughts about Nikhil seemed to occupy a potent corner of my mind. He was everywhere in my life – in my inbox, notes, and prayers. I was getting crazier about him with every passing day but chose to suppress those feelings. He proved to be a subtle lover. He never tried getting down below the belt. For days all we did was have lengthy talks, opening up our hearts, exchanging random kisses and making mute promises which we longed to keep. Coffee dates at night, followed by long intimate walks, became routine.

"Have you ever thought about marriage?" I asked him randomly over coffee one night.

"I have not, basically for two reasons; first, it's not the right age to think about that, and secondly and more importantly, I don't want to ruin anyone's life. I have never had any inclination for girls and I don't think I can love a girl."

"But…if your mother suggested it?"

"Anu, I've never bothered to think about that, but sure, at some point of time I will have to open up."

"You think she will understand?"

"If she loves me as her son, she should."

"Don't you ever think about how people will react once they come to know about our real selves?"

"We're not born to live with this guilt on our heads. We are painted in a different colour but that doesn't make us any different from others. And there are millions like us, even here in India."

"But everyone lives a false life."

"Accepted. But that decision is always yours to make."

"You think you will get a chance to decide?"

"You should hold onto the chance to decide Anu, it's your life. Your sexual identity is as important as your career or coming to this college and doing this course, or anything else that shapes your life."

I nodded. He was right. I was wrong in negating the truth. "I shudder to think of the day I will have to open up to my family," I said. The very thought made me feel nauseous.

His eyes rested on me, glittering with apprehension. I could sense his uncertainty. He gave a long sigh and said, "If you fear coming out into the open so much, you will have to think of a way to live happily while hiding from everyone. Have you ever thought of that?"

I shook my head sadly. "No...."

He gazed around the room to hide his frustration. "Are you telling me you are afraid of living a relationship in the present because of something that may happen in the future?"

"No way," I said sharply. "I want to live this relationship. All I'm saying is that I'm not prepared for the repercussions if anything happens."

"What's the worst that could happen?" he asked, frustration palpable in his voice.

I had never asked myself that question. I gazed at him blankly.

"Leave all this, let's go for a walk. I know you love a ramble," Nikhil suggested, trying to distract me.

It was a good idea, a thought well placed and timely. We got up and soon the night enfolded us in her forgiving embrace.

"I want to confess something," I said, kicking a stone from the path.

"Sure. It won't be a confession for me but go ahead, it will lighten your burden."

"The day we kissed, I went into the bushes and masturbated," I revealed in a rush.

He merely laughed. "I too, dreamt about you that night."

"And what did you dream?"

"I won't tell you. I'm sure it'll soon become reality."

It was all happening in quick sequence.

"You're lusty!" I joked.

"And you're not?" he said, tossing the ball deftly back into my court.

"I won't allow you to use me," I told him seriously.

"It'll be with your permission, will and consent," he said, guiding me into the college bus and bolting it. Planting himself on a comfortable seat, he turned to me. "For old time's sake…"

I allowed myself to reach up and kiss him. He smiled gleefully, knowing the game had begun. He pulled me against him, one hand on my back, the other clasping my face. I rested my hands on his shoulders.

"You are so challenging," he said, kissing me passionately, and forcing my lips open. I responded with equal passion. "You know what I'm thinking?" he chuckled.

"How would I know that?" My whole body had come alive. I felt the charge pulling me towards him, every nerve reverberating to his touch, every muscle flexing to get closer.

"About us… Do you know you smell sweet?" His nose skimmed my neck as he playfully kissed my shoulder. His lips softly trailed down my neck, planting innumerable kisses on the way. I was breathing and swallowing simultaneously, my blood racing towards the hypothalamus, stimulating the release of love hormones. This beautiful chemistry held me in thrall – of wild, desperate and obsessive love.

He placed his index finger on my lips and slowly dragged it down to my sternum. In an emotional reflex my hands slipped under his shirt, touching his lean belly. His body was as toned as Aarya's. *Such an absurd thought*! It was hard to keep up; my emotions were like breakers smashing against the shore. I could feel my heart thumping, desire taking the place of hesitation and unease. My hand reached under his shirt and moved onto his spine.

"Don't think…just…take…it…off!" he commanded.

I looked into his drunken eyes and slowly took off his shirt. He smiled playfully in a futile attempt to hide his desire. I had my hands on his naked body, looking up at him lustfully as he lay comfortably over me, open to my touch. I was pushing the limits of modesty I had set for myself. It was so tantalizingly good, thundering into the deepest corners of my brain; desire coursing through my blood until every part of me tingled.

"Take me," he whispered, his breathing ragged.

I obeyed without hesitation, kissing, licking and sucking his bare body, moving down to his navel. I felt his high.

"Put your arms around my neck," he said softly.

I did as I was told, tugging at his soft hair, the faint smell of his shampoo in my nose. I rolled my head to one side and smiled at him. He looked great in the diffused light. He smiled back, still unsure of my intentions and willingness. He ran his finger across my face and to push me further into the love game, pulled off my shirt. I lay on the seat, he over me, my torso between his knees.

"Delicious," he murmured, caressing my nipples.

"Mmm…" I moaned in desperate craving. I felt like a goddess with all the compulsions of creation within her. It was a new beginning, the creation of the new me.

His lips moved down to my nipples. Guiding my hand to his groin, he murmured, "Feel it."

I gasped with acute pleasure but gathered enough sanity to say, "Not without protection!"

He laughed softly and stretched out comfortably on the seats, his legs hanging down. I placed a leg between his and rested my head on his chest, our bare bodies kissing each other.

"What are you going to do with me?" I asked teasingly.

"Oh.….there are many possibilities," he murmured, his eyes bright. "You know there are two important elements in love," he whispered into my ear.

"So what are they?" I asked, easing myself on top of him.

"Surprise and excitement; the feeling that this moment cannot be replicated."

"And was I able to give you those?"

He smiled in answer. "From now on, I'll want more and more," he promised.

"It took me so long but at last I've found love, in you." I told him, placing a finger on his lips.

He kissed it, replying in his usual poetic way, quoting Rumi, "*I have come to drag you of yourself and take you in my heart.*"

***

The sky had turned red. The moist breeze blew in gregariously through my window to kiss me. A squirrel played outside. I watched it unwearyingly as it gnawed groundnuts. All my feelings and questions melted into that moment. Everything in life is so transitory, except the moments spent conversing with oneself. Casual moments flashed in memory as I combed my hair with my fingers, pondering these dark familiars. Love had inhabited my body and soul. I was held in thrall, caught between the infancy of things and the addictive charm of youth.

The buzzing of the telephone pulled me from my thoughts. It was Harshit. I bit my lip in excitement. His commanding voice was poisoning. He insisted we go for an eat-out. I was enthralled though I was no foodie. I would not have foregone his company for anything. The thought of being with him fanned my burning desires. Perhaps it is sin to think of anyone so intensely.

'I was thinking of going out. Should I pick you up?' he asked.

'Sure! Any plans or something unknown?" I knew he was always keen on finding new places and experimenting with unknown cuisines. In Delhi such unknown often turned out to be the best of places.

'Old Delhi, what say?'

I could not resist. I had heard that the 'real' Delhi was to be found in its old lanes. And he, of course, brought an irresistible charm. I had believed such things only happened in stories but here I was living them! I was in love, perhaps scarred for life. My clouds, my hopes and my sunshine destroyed me. I waited, trying to subdue the sea of excitement roaring inside me. I had no idea how to get him but neither could I shed my haze of optimism.

'I have a delicious surprise for you,' he yelled from fifty paces away as he came riding in on his bike.

I could feel the space between us shrinking to nothing. I knew that deep down he had a soft corner for me. I raced towards him, arms outstretched like a child as he sat on his bike, laughing. He embraced me with the brightest of smiles, pulling my cheeks playfully and planting an innocent kiss on my cheek. He kissed me! Why did the earth not move under my feet or the sky tremble like my feeble soul? He kissed me! Mighty god, I should have fainted at that moment —I felt completely shaken from my whimsical world. But all I could manage was a smile and a gleam in my eyes to express my acceptance. His touch resonated deep, deep within me. I wanted to drape my arm around his shoulders or clasp his hand and bring it close to my lips. A tender smile still tugged at his mouth.

'The only thing that matters to me is food!' I said anticlimactically, trying to subdue the ferment within me.

'Darling, leave that to me. I will take you to the best places,' he assured me in his poisoning, manly, assertive voice. I slid closer on the motorcycle, my right hand around his belly.

The rambunctious streets of Old Delhi are always a maelstrom of activity, offering a mosaic of sights. I had seldom visited this city within a city, its treasures beckoning like alluring ladies of the night. The treasure strewn streets seemed to add another extension of time and life, where past lives and present dreams met in glorious fusion. It was one of the city's most chaotic and crowded, yet captivating areas, with a bamboozling orchestra of sights, smells and sounds. It hosted dire poverty in the shadow of grand Mughal monuments. Beggars lined the alleys, sitting beside vendors selling fresh lime and cold water; homeless drug addicts smoked heroine *on street corners while others slept alongside street dogs... And the traffic crawled along at Delhi's signature speed. Dilli Gate seemed to witness it all, rich and poor, grand and humble, just as it had over the centuries.*

Old Delhi has its own charm. The smell of kebabs and fresh naan bread hung in the air, fruit sellers huddled in a corner which seemed implicitly reserved for them, and shops lined up selling cheap, secondhand garments. I spotted a procession of men going to offer the last namaz of the day at the Jama Masjid. Everything seemed so crowded, yet in order — each with their designated place — the shops, the buyers, even the beggars, drunkards and drug addicts — all perfectly placed to create an urban mosaic. The shock of being in such a crowded place turned to fascination in an instant.

'You know, this part of the city was known as the 'Garden of Eden', with a canal once that ran right down there...under the centre of this road,' he said, pointing to the crossing near one of the seven gates of Delhi.

His words fought against the snarls of Delhi traffic and the gusty summer wind that accompanied the uncertain weather. His knowledge of architecture and Mughal history was impressive, but his expertise in storytelling was something that was to stay with me. In the midst of the high decibel honking, hula-hula of hawkers, dogs barking, abuses from those throngs fighting for footpath space, his words seemed like unadulterated honey. I was so close to him I could smell the delicious, earthy aroma of boyhood leaping towards manhood on his skin.

Harshit parked his bike. Compelled by the traffic, we traversed the length of the famous street on foot. We wound our way like serpents, jumped over puddles and dodged scooters going the wrong way. Autowalas screamed at the top of their voice as the sun burnt out its last fury and evening descended. A flight of pigeons flew past, disturbed by our encroachment into their space. At times Harshit held my hand to help me keep up as he moved swiftly, smiling at my trepid, self-conscious steps.

We passed the Seesganj Gurudwara and I bowed to Nanak Sahab.

'Shall we go?' he asked, pointing to the gurudwara. I nodded. 'This is one of the nine historical gurudwaras of Delhi and it was here that Guru TeghBahadur was beheaded,' he told me. Surprisingly, I knew that. 'This was established by Baghel Singh, a Sikh military leader who marched to Delhi and forged an agreement with the Mughal Emperor Shah Alam II, to establish gurudwaras at historical sites across Delhi.'

I could only nod my head, surrendering myself to his charm and knowledge. I had never been to a gurudwara before. He was far more of a religious guy than me. 'So was Guru TeghBahadur's body cremated here?' I asked.

'Oh no, that's actually contrary to what people believe. Defying the Mughal authorities, the Guru's head was taken by his disciple, Bhai Jaita, to Gurudwara Sisganj Sahib in Anandpur Sahib in Punjab and cremated there. But yes, here you have the trunk of the tree under which Guru Sahib was beheaded.'

'How do you know all this? Do you follow Sikhism?' I asked in wonder, rolling my eyes at him.

He shook his head, his expression lightening immediately. 'Do you need to follow or practice something to know about it?' he retorted, his beautiful smile clouding my senses.

He knew a great deal about the area, not just the best places to eat and the short-cuts, but also the history. The magical silhouettes of the gurudwara spoke for itself. The chaos outside and the serenity within, seemed so perfectly interwoven.

'I will always want to revisit this place,' I said, surprising myself.

'I have more surprises for you,' Harshit said and my heart lurched.

We took a complete tour of Chandni Chowk that evening; had delicious food in cubby-hole places and peeked into allies as he parroted their names. My belly felt like an inflated balloon. The beautiful kaleidoscope of the Great Indian Bazaar added to the fever I had felt at the start of this outing. These unforgettable moments with him made my day. I wished I could have it all in a bottle to amuse myself.

He halted for a smoke. His dominant gaze held me in submission. Strange thoughts confused my mind. The most sacred spaces of my soul were being infested with desire. I could feel it as the blood rushed through my body. I combed my hair with my fingers and looked in the opposite direction to disengage myself from him. I felt hot and cold at once. I would have willingly surrendered to any demand that day; if only he had asked. I wondered whether he even wanted me but did not want to break the spell, wanting to remain in a state of enchanted delirium, with his hypnotic smile titillating me. I wanted to hold the night.

'You want something more?' he asked with a hospitable smile.

'More? Boss, I'm already overfull,' I said dreamily.

'Save some space for dessert,' he said, knowing I had never been a calorie conscious guy. 'Let's go to Jalebiwala; it's close by.'

My mouth twisted into an exultant smile as I said, 'I'm all yours'.

'How about another well thought out eat-out, another date with history somewhere,' he asked, smiling conspiratorially.

Questions erupted like a volcano in my mind but before I could say anything, he put an arm over my shoulders, giving me a half hug and saying, 'Let's go!'

I was a living cauldron of desires — the poetic call of my lonely heart responded to his voice like a mantra. I followed him through the hustle-bustle of the old city, finally climbing into a rickshaw.

'You look so cute when you smile, kid,' he teased.

I beamed. Such feel-good words should have been labelled sinful. 'You are flirtatious,' I mumbled.

'So you think I am flirting with you?' he asked brightly.

'I don't know, but I would love you to,' I responded.

He looked at me with a surreptitious look and my cheeks flushed with pleasure. His closeness made adrenaline course through my body at unimaginable speed.

'Where are you?' he asked, disengaging me from my meditation.

'Nowhere....just nothing,' I stammered, disengaging myself from the serpentine embrace of the desire curling in my belly. The spell was broken and the chaos on the street rang afresh in my ears.

'Well then, we have reached the famous shop for our dessert, a delicacy to end this food trail.'

End...how I hated that word. But then, everything does come to an end sometime.

'You said you were all mine today, so do as I say and try this.'

We shared the jalebis and rabri — ooh, sweet sinful calories...

'Thanks for the day,' I said as we returned to the spot where we had left the bike.

'Thanks for the company. It's good you don't have a girlfriend, I can ask you out anytime I want,' he laughed.

'Don't kid yourself. I could be missing out on many things,' I said.

'Such as?'

'A lot like love,' I murmured, feeling suddenly shy.

He grinned and the conversation I wanted to initiate died. 'Hmm...but didn't I make you feel sexy that day in class?' he murmured naughtily.

My heart gave a jerk. I held on tightly as we drove along, lost in the delicious smell of his hair. I was in a whimsical state, living drunken nights and cloudy days.

When I returned home, I had no answer for my mother who asked where I had been. Instead, I headed straight to my room and fell on my bed. I was living a dream. I knew I loved him from the first moment I saw him. It had been six months now, a long six months spent catching glimpses of him, praying on every rainy day that we would be the only ones in class, silently loving his smile, spending hours watching football, to see him. Lost in his thoughts I scribbled:

Hue of a thousand daisies, embellishes your face,

Your melliferous words make my heartbeats race.

The captivating smile and the passion you wore,

Your elegance, your charm made my feelings soar.

Your smile, like the promises of a moon, excites me,

Your deep eyes, with the calmness of a lake, incite me;

The radiance of your eyes makes the moon shame,

I have realized, I am deep into this love game ....

I hummed the lines feeling like the lonely night waiting for the silver moon to complete it, or an endless sea in search of the horizon. I knew no other dreams would disturb me, no other thoughts linger in my memory, or other images flash before my eyes, from then on. Thoughts of him were to occupy and fill me.

*****

8
DHRITI'S UNCERTAINTY

Sometimes silence becomes the loudest sound and the mind a platform for motley emotions, thoughts, sighs and dreams. I sat on the steps leading to the main college building, an avalanche of emotions welling within. I was alone. I had walked out of the college chaos to find a place to ponder.

"So you're here! I've been looking for you all over the college," Dhriti announced, pulling me from my reverie. "I wanted to ask you something."

"Hmm…" I temporized, a thunderstorm raging within me.

She came to sit beside me. Putting her hand on my shoulder, she said, "Anuj, are you listening? I want to talk to you about something."

"Sure Dhriti, here I am." My voice had a calmness I certainly did not feel.

"Can we talk here or should we go out?"

"Well, if you want to treat me, I have no objection to that," I said smiling blandly.

Her company seemed the very thing I needed in that moment, when life seemed to be flailing around me. The sun had taken the day off. Flocks of birds were making their way back to their nests. They too, were taking the day off.

"Anuj, I know you know about Aarya and me, so I thought it would be good to talk to you. I am rather confused about it all. You know he is so unlike me," Dhriti said as we walked towards the main gate, some five hundred meters downhill.

"But what makes you so uncertain about him?" I asked in an all-business tone, rolling up my sleeves.

"He doesn't sound serious about the relationship. I like him but I've faced all this before. I don't want to go through that shit again. Relationships break before they mature these days," she said all in one breath.

I listened patiently, then blew out a deep breath. "I understand. We often keep such incidents in our memory only to associate them with other experiences."

She looked perplexed, as if repeating my words in her mind.

"By associating moments and events, we often make that the basis of our decisions. You are probably doing the same."

"And may I ask you what makes you think so," she asked with a salubrious smile.

"I believe certain incidents bring back to life moments and events long gone. They are carriers of the past. Don't you feel moments of *déjà vu?*"

"I agree to a certain extent," she said.

"Well, you know, I do think we compare moments and set aside logic. This is just a manifestation in the mind and has no reality in the present. Now may I ask, is it the fear of going through the same emotional battles or the good-for-nothing personality of Aarya that is holding you back from accepting the truth that you have a soft corner for him?"

"Perhaps both, I'm not too sure. By the way, I have never used the term good-for-nothing for him," she said severely.

I loved the reassuring, warm look in her eyes. "You are answering yourself. If it is coming from past experiences, you have reason to rethink but never paint all men with the same brush. And if it is Aarya's personality, let me assure you I have seen deep love for you in his eyes."

We had reached the main gate and we both waived our hands for an auto to stop.

"I will have to strain my sensory nerves again," she joked. "But you have still not given me enough to reassure me."

"You know what you want. While past experiences do hold the immense power to influence the present, frankly, I feel we shouldn't let ourselves be controlled by such thoughts. Experiences should always be lived anew, with fresh vigour."

"So you say I shouldn't think about my past experiences?"

"Yes. By the way, may I ask what those past experiences were?" I asked out of compulsive curiosity.

"Leave all that. It was the same old story — mix-up and break-up. I got more involved than I should have. Now I feel I am more mature."

"Yes, you are. One more question: Why do you doubt this relation when you are already deeply involved?"

"Well…involved as in?" She glanced at me anxiously, knowing that I knew.

"Like…your first kiss?"

She turned pink, perhaps from surprise. But her eyes spoke her displeasure. "You know!" she cried furiously.

"He's my room-mate and a dear friend," I said as a peace offering.

Suddenly a shy smile dawned on her face. "It didn't take me long to fall for him…"

I smiled back. "It didn't take me long to fall for him either. He's a great guy. You will never regret it. Don't over-think it."

"But I am still confused. I like him but I don't know if I am ready for this. Do you think I should spend some time pondering over this?" she asked.

"Is that previous guy still in your life in some way?" I asked, rather nonplussed by her reticence.

"I'm not sure about him either," she said, shrugging her shoulders and giving me one of her rare smiles.

We had reached the coffee house. I wondered what else she wanted to talk about. I knew she regarded me as a confidant. "You don't look happy," I commented, seeing the faint crease between her brows.

"It happened so fast. I don't think I was prepared but neither could I resist. Do you think it's good for me?"

The same old lady's question! I wanted to bang the table and ask, 'Why did you go to his room, taking all that risk, if you were not prepared?' But avoiding the real issue through lengthy conversation is often easier.

"The fact that you did let it happen says you were prepared. If not, you would have resisted." She smiled at this explanation.

"Do you still have questions in your mind? If you keep asking yourself questions, you will never have time to answer. What you are looking for – questions or answers? Okay, for a minute, rewind to those moments you spent with Aarya. If they were good, see how you can repeat them; if they weren't, call Mr. Ex."

She smiled again, whispering "Thanks!" as she put her hands over mine. She changed the topic saying casually, "So, how is your tennis going? You must have learnt a lot by now."

"It's going well. Nikhil is a good tutor, very meticulous, gets into the very basics of the game – the hand movements, the eyes, the swing of the ball, direction, the curve, wind velocity… everything. He's very good," I told her, my blatant admiration having little to do with Nikhil's tennis prowess.

Dhriti took a sip of her coffee. "You know what, I find him rather weird. Maybe weird is not the right word, but he is different. I could be wrong, but don't you feel he is overly friendly with you? Do you hug your friends every time you meet? The ironical thing is he is not an overtly friendly guy in general. In fact, he is quite reticent."

My heart did a quick flip-flop but I chose to laugh off her remarks. "There is a difference between a friend and a tennis partner. He might not be among my closest friends, but for those two hours, during a tennis match, he is the most important person in my life."

"Only a player can understand, you say? Otherwise, he seems a pretty decent guy, and cute too." She batted her eyes.

I smiled. "I hope Aarya does not have a competitor in him."

"Only if you are ready to spare two minutes of your two hours to speak my heart to him." We both grinned in delight.

"And what will I get in return?"

"In return, I can be your stand-in to tell the person you like about your feelings." She took another sip of coffee before saying, "You should not have tried hiding it from me, my friend."

"Hiding what?" I blurted, my heart beating like crazy.

"That you feel something for her…Niharika," came the instant reply.

"I…I…" I was completely flummoxed.

"It's always on your face, the way you look at her, the way you talk to her…everything. Your every action says you like her. Stop hiding it; your feelings are obvious," she revealed.

"But I *don't* think of her that way! She is great company and always a help, but…"

"Really! That's a little hard to believe. She seems so easy with you. Trust me, you will make a good pair. And you have everything a girl would die for – compassion, understanding, good looks, and intelligence.'

My phone buzzed. It was Nikhil's message: *Where are you? I came to your room thinking you would be alone.* I quickly typed: *I'm out with Dhriti.* I looked up. Dhriti was still waiting for a reply. "I never thought of her that way," I said defensively.

"Then who do you look at thaaaat way?" she asked mockingly.

The mobile buzzed again. It was Nikhil's reply: *You could have at least told me before making plans. You should keep this time for us."*

"Aah…no one," I stammered.

She looked at me suspiciously. "The girls are very pretty in our college," she commented suggestively in a low tone.

I smiled, thinking to myself, the boys are even better! There was silence between us then my phone buzzed again: *I am sorry, I am getting too possessive, but I can't help it, I want you. Please come. I am waiting for you....mwaaah.* I smiled to think that anyone could be so helplessly desperate to meet me.

"Someone close?" Dhiriti asked, seeing me smile.

"Oh nothing…just a joke from a friend. Is there anything else you would like to talk about or shall we go?" I asked.

Dhriti looked at me in surprise but finished her coffee and asked for the bill.

***

Where are you? I messaged Nikhil. *My room. I am alone.* ☺ he messaged back. In a few minutes I was there.

"Here comes my baby!" Nikhil said cheerily as I entered the room, a big smile on his face. "Never forget to put on the latch," he reminded me, locking the door and taking me in his arms. "How was your meeting with your friend?" he asked, his eyes cool and assessing.

"It was fine. I'm sorry I made you wait."

He grabbed my waist and pulled me up against him. "Yes, you did..." he said, bringing his mouth close to mine.

"Not now Nik!" My voice sounded harsh as I pushed away. "Not every time we meet...surely we can abstain sometimes." I moved away from him.

Nikhil's mouth dropped open in shock. He stared at me, trying to figure out what I had just said. I stared back, my eyes dull. He moved closer, staring down into my eyes. "But I thought you loved it," he said.

I couldn't keep a straight face any longer and grinned like an idiot. "Fool! I love you!"

He narrowed his eyes at me. My laughter dried up before the forbidding look on his face. He held my shoulders firmly and said, "You know I don't like such jokes." Deadly serious, he looked pissed. My face turned pallid. "Gotcha!" he laughed and kissed me hard.

I clung to his toned body. "Is this all you want from me?" I whispered.

"I want you for all my life. Can you remain mine for that long?" he breathed. Abruptly he released me. "You didn't answer."

I smiled but in my subconscious I was quailing. "Your question is enough to make me live two lifetimes in one," I answered, words coming from my mouth like poetry.

He kissed me hard again, his tongue rolling over mine. "That was for your smart mouth," he whispered in my ear. "Is everything alright? You don't seem to be enjoying my company today."

"I'm tired," I murmured with a half-smile.

"You should take better care of yourself." The welcome words of concern came from him in a rush. "Are you in the mood for it or would you prefer to go out?" he asked.

I failed to understand what 'it' represented. Seated on the bed, he pressed his knee against my thigh and pulled me against him. I should have run from there, but I could not. I did not have the appetite for love that day but neither could I hold out against his desire. His looks went from dark to smouldering. My inner demons drew me towards him at an elemental level.

"I wanna tie you up and have senseless sex till we drop from pleasure," he said, his fingers running across my face, his body hard against mine.

"Yesss…" I replied, my body tightening and responding to the lust in his eyes. Succumbing to his demands I prepared to have him in me. Darkness descended on my mind. Nothing existed except our nude bodies. It was the first time my sexual demands had found an echo. "Niku, I want you….." I cried in pleasure. I placed my hands on his nipples, amazed to see how hard they were. I slowly let my hand slide over his back.

"Let's break our virginity today," he said.

I realized then that it was his first time as well. He pulled me closer. This was what I had dreamt of. The excitement was more than I could stand. He rolled over so he was on top. My body felt alive with electrical impulses. I closed my eyes, beginning to sweat. I could no longer hold myself. The next moment he lifted my legs and placed them on his shoulders; he briefly cupped my round buttocks, spanking them playfully. He pushed in and was soon coming inside me. I could feel every inch of him in and about me. He was gentle, cornering all thought and emotion. His image became imprinted in the deepest layers of my mind, leaving an indelible mark on my life. He was right; we had senseless sex till we dropped from pleasure.

"We should have some dinner," he suggested.

"Hmmm…" I rose and got dressed. "Are you in the mood to get up and go out for dinner?" I asked, throwing his clothes towards him.

"I wanna stay here with your scent," he grinned.

"You can stay with the scent at the dinner table too," I responded.

"You go. I wanna take a bath first."

"Oh, so you want to get the scent off you?" I joked, expecting a quick rejoinder, but he only smiled.

"I'm going to dinner," I said, turning to go. "And no walk today; I have an assignment to do."

***

Aarya and Dhriti were waiting for me at the dinner table.

"Where were you the whole day?" Aarya asked.

"I was with Dhriti, then in Nikhil's room, chatting. We didn't play tennis today. He didn't feel like it so we just sat and shared stories." I tried to smile away the query.

"Don't even suggest you were with me!" Dhriti hissed accusingly. "You left in such a hurry I couldn't even make out what happened! I hope everything is fine? I asked Aarya, but he too, had no clue."

"Boss, you went missing after class. I hope we won't have to hire an investigating agency the next time," Aarya remarked.

"But what's the urgency?" I asked, taking a seat.

"Friends only search for each other in an emergency? I just said we were missing you. The rush in which you left Dhriti made us worry." Aarya tried to hide his real concern behind his casual words.

"Thanks but there is nothing to worry about." I took a slice of cucumber from Aarya's plate.

"I was very sure there was nothing to worry about or you would have told me. It's just that Dhriti was concerned about you," he said mendaciously, pointing to Dhriti with a look that said, 'girls always do that'.

I smiled and got up to go and get my dinner from the buffet. There was fresh salad, something cooked some way, which they called green vegetable curry, and a yellow dal, more diluted than the milk they gave us every morning. I made frequent visits to home to get my nutritional supplements; always bringing back something for Aarya too.

"Anu, we have a rather complicated question to put to you. In fact, we have differing ideas on this," Dhriti said as I returned to the table and sat down.

"Well that's nothing new. You two have different thoughts on everything." I grinned at them but I was on my guard.

"That's not true. We tend to have similar opinions but our perspectives differ," Dhiriti clarified with her usual acumen.

"Two difficult words; you seem to have learnt the language of advocacy and media very well. Anyway, what is the question?"

"It's regarding today's class on morality in the media. Who should decide whether the content is moral? Everything is expression but the media cannot have opinions; that has to be left to the wider audience. At the same time, is media then the side-kick? Should it not lead opinion? So who decides?" Dhriti briefed me in her usual investigative manner.

"Let me narrate a story," I said in reply. "There was an old man who had lived in a small hut for years. His neighbours knew him well. He saved every rupee to live his dreams — of having his semi-*kaccha* hut cemented, white-washed and brightly lit. He wanted to build a small but beautiful life for himself with his savings. One day, when both the moon and the sun hung in the sky, his hut caught fire. All the man's savings and dreams went up in smoke. He sat smiling as he watched the flames engulf his little hut. A neighbour, who had been trying to put out the fire, was stunned by the man's reaction and asked, 'Why are you smiling? You have lost everything!' The old man looked at him without surprise and said, 'I lived in that hut for years, built it brick by brick; everything inside was brought from my savings. I wanted all that once but now I have burnt the hut and everything in it.' Unable to understand, the neighbor asked him the reason for burning down his own hut. The old man looked at him with deep, calm eyes and said, 'Now I have nothing to lose. I have earned my freedom.'"

Aarya and Dhiriti had been listening patiently to the story. Now I put the question to them: "So what would *you* call it – a loss or a gain?"

"It depends how you want to take it. Freedom has complicated definitions. This is where different perspectives come in," Dhriti said. Hers was a typical feminist voice – loud, clear, wanting to prove the relevance of the point raised.

"The thing is there are no clear definitions in life. What one sees is not always the reality; schisms exist between how things are and how they are presented," I said, looking at Aarya. He gave me a helpless look, a cloud of confusion on his face.

"Morality is a matter of perspective," I said. "No one has the right to stamp anything as moral or immoral. Rightly expressed, words empower freedom, but there is always a cost attached to freedom. What the old man considered freedom may not be logical to you or me. Maybe things are like that, translucent – not clear, not opaque, just translucent."

Dhriti nodded, listening intently. Aarya was not. "I love that story. I too, should leave Dhriti one day and say 'Now I have nothing to lose, I have earned my freedom!'" Aarya joked, putting an arm around Dhriti's shoulders.

I concentrated on my food, trying to distract myself from their public display of affection.

"All that we experience, think, perceive or conceive is a surreal mixture of fact and fantasy. There are fine lines between the real and the imagined. We hobble through life's experiences, only to realize our existence rides upon interpretations," I told them between mouthfuls.

"Oooh! But still that leaves our topic of discussion open," Dhriti cried, pushing Aarya away.

"Let it be now. He told us about different perspectives…he answered the questions," Aarya averred, holding Dhriti's hand.

I knew he was not the least bit interested in the discussion. "I think you people should go for a walk while I work on my assignment," I suggested. Aarya immediately stood up.

"Look, your tennis partner! He is so cute," Dhriti said in patently admiring tones.

Freshly shaved and bathed, Nikhil wore a half-sleeved linen *kurta* over blue strapped jeans. He looked debonair. I wanted to yell, 'See, that's my boy!' If only I could do that! As he came closer he smiled and waved.

"Looking good, partner," I complimented him, using the term which gave a public name to our closeness. A blink was followed by a smile, deep pleasure in his eyes.

Plato wrote, *Every heart sings a song, incomplete, until the other heart whispers back.* The same had happened with me. I had consoled myself by believing I did not need another person, but my foolish heart always refused to heed such wisdom. I still wonder why we need someone else to make us complete. I have looked at life in theological terms, but never found the answer. I wished life would flow the way I directed.

Now that the thought of sin had ceased to exist, my heart stopped following the old formulations. Deployed without psychological insight, they seemed dogmatic, anachronistic and irrelevant now. I had become a different person, unable to live with yesterday's thoughts and beliefs. Love never fails to give one flight from fears and pre-conceived notions, sometimes precipitating a state of psychological chaos and pain.

*****

9

A Brief Meeting

It was seven in the evening and the sun's long journey had ended. The evening felt pleasant, the soft breeze blowing gently over my face. I walked towards the guard room near the canteen. We had made love there once when Nikhil had bribed the guard. I'm sure he thought Nikhil had a girl. The aroma coming from the guard hut was dangerously tantalising. Balram Chacha was making tea. The steam from the pot rose swiftly, coiling and leaping higher and higher, provoking random thoughts in my mind as it danced like a vagabond between earth and sky, attached yet free.

"Would you like some tea, son?" Balram Chacha asked.

"Yeah sure. It would be bliss in this weather. Winter is coming," I responded.

"The days are getting shorter and the nights chilly," he said, adding more science to my casual words.

I looked around, holding the beaker he handed me. I had wanted to be free of the college crowd and the unending discussions for a while. Since Nikhil was not in college, my evenings were unoccupied. I chose to go for a lonely silent walk towards the guard hut. I became aware of the stillness and unbroken silence of the place.

"Hi! What a great place to find you!" The silence was broken. It was Niharika, a senior.

"I came for a walk and then just settled in here. Balram Chacha was telling me old stories about the college," I replied, surprised to see her but happy to have some company.

"Stories! My luck has obviously brought me to the right place. This lazy ass rarely steps out for a walk, you know."

Balram Chacha offered her some tea and a toothless smile. She happily accepted, the hot tea beautifully complementing the chilly evening.

"This part of the college is very nice – green, silent and still," she said, her bright eyes gazing into the darkness. "Do you come here often?"

"Not often, but I do sometimes come here on a ramble. It's a nice place, away from that madding crowd and the frustrating discussions on the same old topics." Although I had spoken to her before, this time I felt bewitched by her eyes.

"Have you ever been down to that short stretch of grassland that goes downhill?" she asked, pointing.

"A few times. I've heard it is home to migratory birds."

"Yes, try going on a bird trek, from the grassland to the lake area. I can guarantee you will find at least twenty species. In my first year I was quite a pepped up adventure girl and photography enthusiast. I often trekked down that path with my camera."

I searched for a suitable expression and foolishly chose a bland look. "Twenty is quite a good number of species," I remarked.

"Yes it is. I have been to other places like Okhla Lake too, but the environs here are quite condusive to freaky souls. There are many hidden spots, though most are used for purposes they are not meant for." She rolled her eyes and Nikhil's hideouts for love-making brought a smile to my face.

"Every place should be put to the best possible use. And people do love to use spaces differently." I punctured her sarcasm with my devil's advocate reply.

"Let live. I know how I use the hideouts," was the quick retort.

"Before you came, Balram Chacha was telling me the story of this dark road — *Andheri Gali*," I said, sparking a wave of enthusiasm in her.

"So what is the story, Balram Chacha?"

"Oh nothing…there is no sense in repeating it," he replied, giving his signature toothless smile.

"Do you know why this road is a cul-de-sac leading nowhere?" I asked.

"Perhaps a planning error which enabled many lovers to plan their lives?" she suggested, blowing out a misty breath.

"Actually, the academic block building was supposed to be on this side, but before construction could begin, strange things started happening and that's why the design was changed and hence this cul-de-sac," I stated calmly.

"Strange things like what?" she whispered, caught by my words.

"For instance, they found many dead birds on this road, and the trees had shed their leaves long before autumn. Some people even complained they had heard strange sounds." I narrowed my eyes speculatively. Niharika remained tight-lipped.

"Not just that, all the street lights on this road stopped working one night. They were replaced the next day and they worked. But, towards midnight a few days later, they stopped working again," Balram Chacha added for good measure.

"But did anyone see anything?" I asked.

"No and no one was harmed in anyway. But we were certain that some supernatural power did not wish the building to go up here," he replied, myriad emotions crossing his face as memories sprang to life.

"And when did all this happen?" Niharika asked.

"A few days after the laying of the foundation stone... there was a lot of tension then and no one talks about those days now. Even I have heard strange voices."

"Chacha why did all this happen do you think?" Niharika asked, taking a final sip of tea.

"Who knows? But all activity was stopped and today the site is part of the grassland – lying unutilised."

"Calling it unutilized would be incorrect. It's been put to different uses and the ghosts seem to have no issues with those," Niharika commented astringently.

"Perhaps the ghost is voyeuristic," I remarked.

She giggled delightedly. "Nice story over a nicer cuppa. Now I don't regret my decision to go for a walk."

"If you had not, you would never have known this story."

It was dark and the mosquitoes had started buzzing around. She smiled, nodding her head. "Don't think too much about it. Whatever happened is in the past."

"But the story is interesting. For a second, assume it is true. We are probably on haunted ground." I blinked at her.

"Then may God forgive us our trespasses," she said in an alarmed voice, sounding ridiculously tense.

"Okay, I'll take your word for it that the past is in the past. But the next time I go there, this story will float in my head."

"And will you go there to know the place better or on different pursuits?" she asked.

"Curiosity killed the cat, my dear."

"You know, you can be very obtuse," she chuckled.

My lips twitched. "All that apart, I will go for a bird walk with you to the lake one day, right through the grassland, saying hi to our voyeur ghost," I replied.

"That sounds like a plan. I shall wait for that day to be off to the urbane wilderness," she smirked. "Stop by for a chat over coffee some time. We still have loads to know about each other," she added, turning away towards the girls' hostel.

"That would certainly be a nice sweetener for our coffee," I said, waving goodbye and going towards my hostel. I could not somehow forget those bright, stormy eyes!

Putting my hands into my pockets, I sauntered towards my room. In the large mirror on the bathroom wall, I gazed at my face. I looked unusually pale, gaunt and famished. She was right, there was a hard, obtuse look about my face. As I hurried to take a hot shower, hoping to rid myself of my blues, I couldn't help imagining Nikhil in the shower with me. We had never tried it.

Aarya was not in the room. I felt transported to some lone island by the tranquility of the night. The college was unusually quiet. I checked my phone – no messages from anyone. Nikhil had gone to his hometown and my evenings felt empty and lifeless without him. I missed him. I felt myself pushed towards a cave of dark solitude. In desperation I called Aarya. "Where are you? I'm alone and bored," I complained.

He laughed. "You sound like a kid asking his daddy to come home early. I've already entered the hostel gates; will be there before you put your phone down."

I put down the mobile, feeling desperately lonely.

"Heyy kiddu!" Aarya yelled from a distance. He was loaded down with shopping bags. "What happened?" he asked, trying to hide his amusement.

"I was just feeling lonely."

"Well, get dressed, we're going out," he announced.

"We?"

"We as in 'many people'. We are going to the food festival. Basically the three of us, perhaps joined by a few others," Aarya announced, narrowing his eyes.

I laughed at my own stupidity. I had completely forgotten about the food festival.

"Lord! So at last you've remembered we had decided to go. The only difference is that now, instead of three people, there will be fifteen." Aarya casually mentioned this critical piece of information before turning away to drop his packages.

"I have no issues with that, but you'll probably get no time with Dhriti," I reminded him.

*****

10

FIRST FIGHT AND A HEAVY PRICE

We chose a small intimate restaurant.

"Look at this place!" Nikhil grumbled.

The place seemed suited to the rough conversation we were about to have. Nevertheless, it was cozy, had wooden chairs, linen tablecloths, quick service and was well within our budget. Nikhil was not overwhelmed, being quite meticulous in his dining choices and ridiculously nerdy about the cuisine. To me it seemed a fitting choice and frankly, I would have abhorred a romantic setting with flowers to discuss, or rather quarrel over, what was upsetting me.

We sat staring at each other in silence, without the usual compassion. Desire for him, adulterated with an element of revulsion, was close to the surface. I could see my desire-revulsion reflected in his eyes. I closed my eyes, mortified. 'I am not his slave,' I thought. 'I do not have to tell him everything I do. He cannot tell me what to do or who to talk to.' And so the soliloquy continued…

"We don't have much time," Nikhil finally said.

"We have enough time to talk," I retorted, my voice cracking. The pain of not being given the respect you deserve is greater than any physical pain. Hurt flowed through me. He had been acting like a control freak, questioning my activities, demanding every little detail of my whereabouts and almost deciding my daily schedule.

He looked at me, strain in his eyes – the pain of being challenged. The slave had spoken and the master in him felt challenged. The silence was broken by the tinkling of his spoon against his glass – deafening to my ears.

The waiter approached with a menu, handing us a much needed pause. "Would you prefer Indian or Mughlai?" he asked.

Ooooh…they served Mughlai! Instantly my sensory nerves were on alert.

"We'll go through the menu and let you know," Nikhil said passively to the waiter.

"Call me when you are ready to order Sir," the man responded, leaving us alone to argue.

"Anu, you behave like a kid sometimes," Nikhil sighed, the agony of the defeated prince in his voice.

"It's not about being a kid but being allowed to be an adult," I replied in a venomous voice.

"Who is not letting you be that?"

"You know the answer, Niks! You know the reason for my surly behaviour." I was getting loud.

"This is a public place," he reminded me.

"Sorry," I answered in a sullen tone.

"Would you like to try some Mughlai today?" he asked, raising his eyebrows at me expectantly, arrogance personified. He knew very well that I loved Mughlai.

"Okay, but you choose," I said, offering him something like an olive branch.

To my surprise, he ordered only vegetarian dishes, infuriating me! Good food would have served to calm my anger. The waiter retreated to the kitchen. I looked at Nikhil and frowned, saying nothing. He was vexed, something was eating him – perhaps it was me. But then it was he who had brought things to this pass. He had crossed the invisible lines I had drawn in my mind. There are things that are acceptable while other things confound you. His actions did the latter. Though my inner goddess was rising sleepily, stretching to accept him, absolving him of all misdemeanours and nonsensical acts, something kept me dithering, holding her at bay.

"You are a grumpy little cat," he accused, pressing his lips together.

"I wonder why you would say that? I have always wanted to set the right tone for an honest relationship. You keep missing your lines. You cannot be so churlish with me, Niks. Why must I always listen to you or you decide for me – what to eat, who to meet, my clothes, the books I read, my English, my Hindi, my time with Aarya…every damn thing! Have you ever wondered how I feel being restrained and watched to that extent? In simple words, you are trying to micro-manage my life." I found myself falling short of words.

His lips pressed together to hide a smile. "I decide for you because I love you," he answered in a low voice attuned to the public space we were in.

I could see the intimacy and honesty in his eyes but discarded the thought. A simple, honest reply to let him get hold of the strings of my life…never! "Things don't run that way Nikhil. No one wants a guy with a remote control. I'm not a toy which you can set dancing to your tune. It would get more and more stifling for me as time passes. And what would others say if they get a hint of this? I fear that a few may have already got more than a hint from the way you treat me. You cannot compel me to follow you. I am your lover, but also a person; not something to command and call to your bed," I fumed, venting my frustration and pain.

The waiter brought us plates and scuttled away. *Food*…it was the last thing on my mind at that moment. I was hungry but sitting with the person I loved, discussing the uncertain future in a mindful conversation about mutual respect and trust, tended to kill the appetite. I looked dubiously at the plates.

A brief silence followed. The waiter was back with dinner. It smelt delicious. He served us and gingerly filled our glass with water before beating a hasty retreat. Even he could sense all was not well.

"I'm sorry, but you know I'm not wrong. Let's have dinner. We have the whole way back to discuss, or not, this thing." I tried to smooth over the situation while retaining the dominant hand in the conversation.

"I still do not get why you are so bugged."

"There are reasons Mr. Control Freak." I don't know how I managed to say those words. I had never spoken to anyone with such direct candour. It was an honest confession requiring grit – something I usually lacked.

He ran his fingers through his hair, his gaze intense and disarming. He looked at me and then fixed his attention on his meal. "That's quite a character sketch," he said.

"I'm sorry. I shouldn't have used those words."

"Apology accepted but it does seem childish."

There it was again – the all-knowing master and the naïve student. We ate in silence. I stole a glance at him to judge his mood, trying not to let him know I was doing so. Perhaps he was doing the same, knocked off-balance by this behavioural aberration in me. His passive, supple, tame, submissive creature had stopped purring for him. It hurt his superman ego. His glare had darkened to something sinister. I could see he was boiling with silent wrath.

"The food is good here," he said, breaking the dead silence between us.

"Uhmm…" I chose not to foster his efforts at normalcy.

"What is your problem?" he asked, his frown deepening. He was bristling with his barely controlled anger. I was not playing to his rules; the control he had practiced over me was suddenly waning.

But one needs to choose for oneself. I had chosen to live the relationship on terms of mutual respect and not let him waltz in and do just what he wanted. "You must stop trying to intimidate me, Niks. I don't want anyone directing me. You cannot control me, damn it!" I said in a low voice that shook. The public place we were in compelled me to stifle the intensity of my emotions.

"Do I?"

"Yes!"

He turned towards the waiter and asked for the bill, ignoring my fervent words. There was deep displeasure in his eyes, his face frigid. "I know you are angry and that doesn't make for a healthy discussion. Something must have gone wrong between us, but it cannot be a reason to end everything," he said, his tone accusatory.

"I am *not* ending everything. I am saying something needs to change if are to continue. All this time I have tried being whatever you wanted me to be. I am surprised we couldn't understand each other's needs better in six months. It's a long time, you know."

"Understand? We did! That is why we are here together."

The waiter arrived with the bill and a smile as we sat looking at each other, filled with unspoken recrimination.

"Hmm…it was cheap," Nikhil murmured. This dinner was on him.

"Good for your pocket," I smiled, finally a lighter moment after an hour of tumultuous conversation.

"Let's go," he suggested and I nodded.

We walked silently towards the place where his bike was parked. He deliberately brushed his hand against mine but I drew away. I wish his love would transcend his ego. Even a look can convey that and I kept glancing at him, hoping. I was never a guy to obey logic, allowing it to tinker with my mind to make the right decisions. I had always hated logic. I am a man who obeys emotion and seeks expressive words and glances to brighten moments.

"You should know how to communicate and let others know of your feeling. You should have made me realize how you felt when it started, instead of now, when it has become unbearable for you," he snapped.

"Why is it always I who has to learn or know things? Why not admit that you too, failed to realize it and straighten out things?" I replied, stung.

It was a blow to his pride and he scowled. "I take it that every fault is mine," he whispered menacingly.

"It takes understanding to hold onto a relationship," I reminded him.

"The problem arises when understanding evaporates and accusations take its place," he snapped.

"I admit I am equally to blame," I said in a snubbed voice, my heart constricting.

"I hope your love still exists and has not changed." He sounded uncharacteristically vulnerable.

"That cannot happen," I assured him. I yearned to break ranks and hold him tight, saying sorry, sorry…

He looked relieved as he exhaled. "Good. Let's go straight to the hostel."

I glowered and stalked off towards the bike. It took us barely ten minutes, the traffic having eased. Nikhil parked in the parking lot and forcibly dragged me towards the academic lot. A narrow pathway led towards the faculty area. He quickly glanced up and down the dark alley before abruptly pushing me against the wall. Grabbing my face between his hands, he forced me to look into his determined, controlling eyes. He crushed himself against me so suddenly that it allowed me only a short gasp of protest, which evaporated as I realized what he was up to.

"If you think I control you, then so be it. I will keep doing that," he whispered fiercely.

I gasped, looking straight into his agonised eyes, displeased, hurt but wanting. His mouth descended hard, demanding, then possessing. He kissed me violently. Our teeth clashed briefly as his tongue rolled pleasure into my body, leaving me feeling loved and wanted. Desire exploded with glorious intensity. Losing myself in passion I matched his violent passion, forgetting my displeasure, kicking aside my tantrums. My hands knit in his hair. I groaned with pleasure, the sound reverberating within me. His hands moved over my body, unlocking my desires. When he lifted his mouth, I felt my soul being drawn to him through his eyes. My hands cupped his face. I was once again letting him control me. Deep inside I wanted this control freak.

"I don't wanna make a habit of apologizing to you, but I can't stop controlling you. It makes me feel you are a part of me," he muttered between short sweet kisses, his lips soft now.

He dominated me and deep down I loved it, realizing it was an expression of protection. I loved being tamed this way. "You don't have to apologize," I said softly.

"I won't; you are mine," he snarled, stressing each word.

I leaned against the wall, panting, trying to control the flash flood of desire and regain emotional balance. "I'm sorry. I think I overacted," I gasped, trying to regain my breath.

He accepted my apology with a gentle kiss, making the moment unforgettable. "I can't afford to lose you."

"We need to understand each other more," I said, pacifying the Venus within. I indulged myself with another kiss. Instantly all my arguments, tantrums, thoughts of personal liberation were lost.

A foggy, starry night and two lovers in the dark, making love to apologize – it couldn't possibly have been more romantic. We made unstoppable love, losing ourselves in each other. Breathless, we coiled into an inseparable embrace. We kissed between smiles and smiled between kisses – in perfect harmony.

"If apologies can be so beautiful, I'd love to keep erring," he said, resting his head on my chest.

***

Tinted clouds, speckled with light, floated lazily across the sky. It was five in the morning and I was taking a walk on the lawn, crushing the dew-laden blades of green grass under my feet. I hated being up so early, that too, on a Saturday. Usually I would be lying happily in bed, listening to the first birdsong in the garden and imaging the dawn swallowing the darkness of night from behind closed eyelids. I would curse the sun for incinerating my dreams.

But today was different. I had set the alarm for five, woken lazily and rummaged for my leather jacket in the closet and then emerged like a brave boy to see the rising sun surreptiously kissing the roses and marigolds in the college garden. Had it not been for Dhriti, summoning me to India Gate, I would still be lost in my dreams. India Gate this early in the morning. Who does that? Only a crazy friend…

It is a state of drifting, she says — doing the oddest things in a wondrous way. She was perfect at it and I loved that about her. She came to know about Nikhil and me long before Aarya even imagined it in his wildest dreams. But she kept it to herself, standing by me through the worst of times, always trying to take me towards fulfillment.

"Sorry I made you wait," she called as she hurried past the palms towards me

"I knew you would be late," I grumbled.

"I'm not the early riser type," she stated unapologetically.

"Then why make such an odd plan?"

"I actually wanted to make it midnight," she told me.

"I have a bike I can borrow."

"I know…Nikhil would never say no to you."

Her words caused a flutter of trepidation in my belly but I smiled and said, "You'll be the first girl to go out with me."

"I'm hardly amazed since girls need to be a priority in your life before they can take a ride with you. That appears to be an impossible task for any girl."

I got the drift but chose not to comment. "So now, since we are up, its better we make a move. By the way, you could have asked Aarya to come too," I said, kick-starting the bike.

"And you think that lazy ass would have got up at six to accompany us? It's better not to ask at all than to ask, get a false assurance, and then be disappointed," was the dramatic reply. I had apparently become her perpetual sacrificial lamb.

"I love the mist. If you aren't strolling in the early winter morning, you aren't living it," Dhriti declared as we made our way out.

"Add to it the fun of biking," I quipped. The breeze had not still shed the chill of night, and the birds were out, embracing the gentle warmth of the sun. Everything seemed unlike the usual bustle of Delhi. School and office timings must have changed. Winter makes everyone later in getting to work and earlier getting home – a reduced work life. We biked our way through the desolate lanes, Dhriti clinging to me for warmth.

"I wish it was some other girl clinging to me," I said provocatively.

"Wish on buddy. You need to get that rolling too; which you don't want."

"How can you say I don't want it?"

"Had you wanted it, I wouldn't be the first girl to be going for a ride with you," she said, her words emphatic and definite.

"You can take the charm out of any conversation," I complained.

"It's not about taking the charm out of conversation; I was just being honest in answering your question. Could be you never got the girl of your choice."

We arrived at our destination. The majestic gate, looking straight at the Presidential palace, the foggy morning, the unusually desolate streets, and us walking on the dew-drenched grass like gypsies, seemed like something straight out of a Bollywood romance.

"It's really charming, I mean the entire scene. I've only come here in the evening, when it's crowded. It is nice when everything is so quiet". I turned to her and asked, "So anything in particular that made you come?" I knew she wanted to talk.

Dhriti tapped the side of her nose and looked at me from the corner of her eye, trying to hide her glee. It was most unlike her. "I didn't have much in mind really. I just thought we could share something we would both enjoy." She looked away, trying to avoid eye contact.

I looked at her, smiling my lopsided grin. *She had something important to say.* "I can truthfully say it was a good idea. I have spent twenty years in Delhi but never came here this early."

"Well, let's find a place for ourselves on the wet carpet," she said, blinking her eyes in excitement. She reached for my hand, which I willingly entrusted to her, and hurried me over the pavements. She turned to me with her 'I'm eighteen' smile and urged, "Come on buddy, faster!"

"Hey, sweet lark, I'm not a sprinter."

"Oh I can outpace you any time. Now come and sit here. Have loads to talk about."

I guessed it was the Aarya saga again. Lucky girl, she could at least share her emotional tittle-tattle with a friend. "Tell me, my dear," I said sounding staid and serious.

"My story is going well," she replied instantly. "You tell me about yourself."

This was unexpected. "Wish I had a story to tell," I answered flippantly, hoping to deflect her.

"You know, I saw you with Nikhil yesterday, in the faculty area, late at night, doing something." Her voice was low, her eyes clouded with suspicion.

I inhaled sharply. The horror of those words left me feeling breathless. My face darkened then turned pale. I was appalled by what she had said but appreciated her decision to speak of it away from the campus. It was clear she wanted to know more.

"You know things?" I asked, almost panting.

"I saw things worth knowing about."

Things had turned ugly in a moment. Silence set in. My eyes met hers; I turned to stare blindly at the iconic monument in all its grandeur.

She gave me an amused look. "I saw what you did."

My subconscious cringed in guilt, embarrassed by this revelation. "You brought me here to tell me this?" I asked sternly.

She grinned goofily at me. "You have great choice by the way."

Her words left me more shocked than the revelation of a moment ago. I flushed with surprise. As my eyes met hers, the guilt receded.

"That guy, that gift to women, loves *you*! You should be congratulating yourself," she told me.

I sat amused and puzzled, looking at her again to assure myself that she was serious and not merely poking fun at me. She looked happy and animated despite what she had come to know about me. I had expected otherwise.

She took my hand in hers. "Don't worry; your secret is safe with me."

I cocked my head to one side and asked quizzically, "You have questions?"

"I had many last night. I thought of calling you to get answers. I was shocked and angry but then I thought of coming here and discovering a concealed chapter of your life, hence the plan…" she said softly, a touch of melancholy in her voice.

My eyes were wet. I don't know whether it was due to regret, her trust, or a new meaning to our friendship.

"I thought about it the whole night, Anuj. It's hard to even imagine what I saw, but it is what it is. That is your reality," she said, eyeing me speculatively.

"Right…it is my reality." I boldly accepted what I had most feared.

"I believe he would look after you well. That's how he seems to me – kind, reliable and loyal. He is a pleasant guy but keeps to himself," she commented dryly.

"What did you think last night?" I asked.

"Nothing much; my brain froze," she said, trying to avoid the question.

"You just said you thought about it a lot."

"Is it important to tell you everything? Some things can just be left unexplained, unanswered. Some memories, visuals, and experiences should just be erased, not brought back." Her lips curled in a wistful smile. "We can talk about something else. I just wanted to tell you that I know."

I took a deep breath. "You could have told me all this in college, there was no need to come here. It seems you have something else in your mind that you are not telling me."

"I wanted to let off steam. I was thinking like an old granny last night. It is different this morning. Nothing I thought last night matters now. For me those thoughts are long dead."

I felt winded but nevertheless craved to hear more.

"I had only heard of what I saw last night. You two were intimate. For a moment it seemed like you were made to be together. But then, seeing two guys together like that crippled me the whole night. I thought it couldn't possibly be you. I know you well. But it *was* you."

Gone was the carefree me. My eyes narrowed, my heart thumped and my gut wrenched as she spoke her heart.

"For a moment, I thought as my granny would have – a guy kissing a guy is unacceptable, unnatural." She stopped for a moment to look into my wet eyes before continuing. "I don't know how to put it but I simply couldn't accept that sight."

"Then what made you change your mind today?" I asked, breathing an inward sigh of relief.

"The fact that you are my friend."

"Had I not been?"

"I don't know if I would have given it another thought or accepted the relationship at all. It is too difficult a question to answer. I thought about the kinky fuckry the two of you must be engaging in, but that does not change you for me. I remembered you talking about different perspectives the other day, your old man story. Well you seemed to be that old man to me, ready to set fire to everything he had earned to live free. With that thought my perspective changed. What had seemed shocking began to seem acceptable."

I smiled, elated to hear it. "If you accept me, you can accept this relationship too."

"Anu, I can't assure you if I'll be able to accept this relationship. You may call me a prude, an old woman, but you I will always accept."

"People are born this way, Dhiriti. It's my life and many others live this life too. You know I once hated myself for being gay, but then realized such an attitude would not let me live."

She rubbed her hands over her thighs, looking uncomfortable. "Anu, you are a dear friend. With you I shall laugh, and for you I shall cry. I am happy you have found someone to love you. My thoughts hold no value and you shouldn't worry over that."

"I hope you will keep this to yourself," I said, looking straight into her eyes.

She looked back at me, an intense look on her face, scrutinizing me. Then she took a deep breath and said, "Sure. I won't tell anyone, not even Aarya."

"Thanks! He should not know."

"He will not get to know it from me. And the fact that I know will not affect our friendship," she assured me.

Her words gave me a new lease of life. I smiled to show my appreciation. "And may I say another thing? I feel no such thing for Aarya."

She bit her lip to stop the laugh that seemed to rise up irresistably and nodded. How difficult it is to be oneself. How would Aarya feel knowing that his room-mate harboured feelings for other guys? These were big questions – about perspectives, my truth, his truth, and the universal truth that negate all else.

"Shall we walk around this place and head towards Raisina Hill before making our way back to the hostel?" she suggested.

There was truly nothing more to talk about. But I felt light. At long last I had opened myself to someone.

"You know I am quite jealous of you," she said, her eyes glowing naughtily. "Still I am happy for you."

I had a smile on my face as we walked together for some time, not talking much. She asked me some random questions about my relationship and I gave her equally random answers. Once the sun began to get hot, we decided to return.

***

I could not meet Nikhil that morning; he had a class to attend. I wished to apprise him about my conversation with Dhriti. Aarya was not in the room; he had gone out to get some stuff. I knew he would be back late. I studied myself in the mirror. I looked pale and strangely blank. I was fine with Dhriti knowing my truth but then a sudden thought occurred to me – what if others had also seen us or knew in some way? What if Aarya got to know? I searched for my phone to send Nikhil a message: *Please meet me when u r free, have something important to tell, m n my room.* Back came his reply: *After class.*

I paced the room, stopping at regular intervals to check my watch. Another hour – the thought was enough to make my heart sink. I felt trapped. I looked at my watch again. Something had fundamentally changed in the last few hours, something in me, something that had brought on this fear. I wanted to drape myself around him and stake a claim on his being. I always felt safe, relieved and excited in his arms; his deep eyes seemed to have the answer to every question.

I tried distracting myself from these thoughts, but I needed him to make my fears evaporate in the heat of his passion. I wanted to hear from him, to be loved by him, to lose myself in him. I just wanted him. I typed again: *You will have to be quick.* He replied: *Why so frisky?* I quickly replied: *It's not good here.*

I walked to the balcony, my mind prickling with apprehension. My heart followed the rhythm of my watch. I didn't know what had changed me so quickly. I had looked straight into Dhriti's eyes and accepted my being, regardless of how she would take it. I had casually assured myself she would keep the truth to herself. Dhiriti had acted as a friend should, promising to keep it to herself. I believed her. Surely this fear did not stem from that episode? Then what? I suppose I had never faced myself more before. I turned and walked towards my bed, deep in delusion. I waited for the knock on the door. The only thing I craved was for him to shake me out of this limbo. I wished he would come and resurrect me with his love. I looked at my watch again…fifteen minutes left.

And he came. I rushed like an eager child to answer his knock. He stood there in his white shirt and blue denims, tall, tanned and lovely with hair shining like a halo. He looked addictive.

"Will you not let me in?" He broke into my addiction.

It was the first time he had been in my room. He did a quick inspection, it wasn't as tidy as his, thanks to Aarya, but then, by hostel standards, it was well enough.

"Now, tell me what is troubling you so much?" he asked, sitting down on my bed.

I sat down next to him, my fearful eyes lifting to his. "Dhriti knows about us. She saw us kissing last night." I waited for his explosive reaction.

He blinked but strangely enough, remained calm and composed. "What was her reaction? If it was good, why trouble me to rush here? Leave it. Tell me about your day."

Was he serious? I was dying that the truth was no longer hidden and he was asking me about my day? Or was it that he was prepared that it was bound to happen someday?

"My day started with this." I bit my lip, my face darkening.

"I see, so this was the cause of so many messages." He tilted his head and smiling in his oh-so-sexy smile.

"So many messages?" I cried, stung. "There were just two! This set the worry bells ringing for me."

"It isn't that big a thing. Someone had to know someday, and it's good that it is Dhiriti. We can be sure it will not turn into gossip over coffee."

I shook my head, my heart in my mouth. I squirmed uncomfortably. "It *is* a big thing, Nik."

"She is your friend; she understands."

I could not understand his cool attitude. Even if it was not a big thing and I was, as usual, worrying too much, he needed to be more concerned? Any sane person would be.

"Someday I will have to open up to others, but that doesn't mean I am mentally prepared for it," I cried.

"You think too much. You think a lot and worry a lot. Everything will be alright."

Had he not seen the way people react on hearing the word 'homosexual' or was he just pretending to be composed? He stroked my chin. "Your eyes become deep brown when you are stressed," he said.

I stared at him, shocked, wondering how to answer. I was so anxious and here he was chuckling. He pressed his lips against my neck, offering solace. I breathed in his scent, my favourite fragrance.

"Hey, don't worry," he said softly.

"Hmm…" I murmured, blinking. "I don't when I am with you, but you know me."

He smiled his heart-stealer smile. "Thanks, and yes, I do…" he whispered.

In a moment I transitioned from worried aunt to desperate lover. My fears evaporated in the blink of an eye, so irresistible was my love for him. Leaning forward, he tilted my head back and trailed kisses of fire down my neck. I moaned with desire, the goddess inside me awakening. The soft, sweet confession of love in his eyes ran through my soul, granting absolution. Tears pricked my eyes. *I need you to fight for me* I whispered in his ear. Every minute with him was like an elixir, short lived yet unforgettable.

It was liberating for fragile, self-contained me to be in the arms of a beautiful man who could have been a character in a romantic novel – the perfect ingredients for a complicated love story with a twisted ending. My tears and his smile wove the story of pain and assurance. I reached forward to clasp his handsome face and kiss him gently. He wrapped me in a gentle, reassuring hug, allaying my fears with his touch. I trailed his shaven chest with my fingers. He smiled as his fingers trailed up and down my spine. So much had happened between us by then. We were always trying to balance the see-saw between us, hiding our desires while expressing them only to ourselves.

"I want you for myself," he said.

I wanted that too. Then who did I fear – the world that would anyway come to know about us? I saw my life with him.

"I won't let you go," he murmured.

We merged into each other. His love was the end of everything old and the start of everything new for me. I was completely enveloped in the desperate desire to be with him, to be his completely, now and forever.

***

I woke from a deep, comforting sleep. Dusk had tiptoed in and the sky was awash with shades of opal and pink perfectly blended and woven together. I looked out; it was a clear, crisp evening, carrying the chill of coming winter. It was going to be a lazy evening for me, spent on the balcony looking at passers-by and reading a novel. No tennis that evening. We had played enough. I wondered what Nikhil was doing; perhaps in the library. I searched for my phone and messaged: *What are you doing?* The reply was almost instant: *In the canteen, having coffee....give me company.* The simple words set off a hormonal rush. I put on my jacket against the chill and set off towards the canteen. There he was in a corner by himself.

"So how was your day?" he asked.

"You made my day so perhaps you should answer that question," I replied with a lopsided grin.

He smiled the oh-so-sexy smile girls sighed over. "If you say so, pal. I've ordered a cup of coffee for you too. Should we order something to eat?"

"Let's go out to eat," I suggested. I wanted the solace of his company.

"That sounds like a plan. We'll have coffee here and then go out for dosa," he announced enthusiastically.

Dosa…I wondered. He loved the flavours of this south Indian dish. I was just hungry for his company, whatever the cuisine involved. My special coffee arrived, steaming hot.

"Niks, you'll be gone in a few months for your internship."

He looked up. "That's not few months, I will be gone in August, till the end of November - and August is nine months away." He took a sip and looked at my morose face. "We have months of happiness, then who knows, I might get an internship here in Delhi. Then I'll take a flat and we can live together like a married couple."

I smiled at the thought of living together. How I longed to live with him, day after day. "That is not allowed in India," I reminded him though deep down I loved his idea.

"Who is coming in to see? It's ironical the law doesn't recognize us, but then, we don't like what the law says either!"

He spoke in a rebellious tone, a store-house of energy. I always lacked that drive.

"But tell me, will you come and stay with me, if that happens?" He threw the ball into my court. I nodded. "So on that beautiful note, let us celebrate with dosa!"

Now that was surely the height of dosa love. I now had two guys to define my life – one always had a tot of whiskey ready, and the other wanted to celebrate every odd and even thing over a plate of dosa. I was surely blessed or cursed.

We set off, walking towards the main gate. I had never imagined romance over dosa. Perhaps he sensed this for he asked, "You want to have this or should we try something else?"

"It fills my stomach and keeps me moving. All I really need is your attention but that's not possible with dosa around," I lamented.

"Hey, why don't you learn to make south Indian dishes before we settle down?"

"Nooo…if I am in charge of the kitchen, I will prepare the dishes of my choice," I replied firmly.

"But I thought my choice was our choice," he quipped with a naughty look.

I looked straight into his eyes and said, "Only when I say so." A short sweet one-liner to settle dues. He lifted a hand to acknowledge a hit, his hazel eyes gleaming.

The dosa place was just about thirty steps from the college gate;

he called it 'luxury at the gate'. It had become one of the most common spots for us to be seen together; the canteen and the tennis court being on the list as well. Had one of us been a girl numerous stories would have circulated around the campus by then. Perhaps it is a luxury of gay love that convention masks love as friendship. But Nikhil was a loner; people who knew him could take our closeness as being odd. He hardly opened up to people; he was compassionate and had a great sense of humour, but he was also an intensely private person. I was an exception. It was enough to raise a few brows. Though I had not come across any gossip relating to us, the way some people looked at us hinted that a story had begun to do the rounds.

***

I have always believed that some stories are meant to be told, but never imagined that mine would be one of them. We returned from dosa hang-out and Nikhil headed for another love — the library. I headed to my room. A little chit-chat with Aarya was warranted. My mobile vibrating distracted me from my random thoughts. It was a message from Nikhil: *I know you curse me for my dosa love.* There was a stupid smiley after the text. I replied with another smiley with a tongue peeping out.

Nikhil had his favourite sections in the library. He was specifically interested in psychology journals. Perhaps his compulsive reading provided the soil for his intellect and sound understanding of human psyche. He took a journal from the shelf and seated himself near a window.

"Hi! May I sit here?"

"Sure," he said, the blood leaving his brain as he looked at the girl before him.

"I am Dhriti, Anuj's friend," she said, wedging herself into the seat next to his.

Though his body felt leaden, he managed to convince himself that this meeting was nothing untoward. "I know," he replied, casting her a long suspicious look.

She returned the stare for a second, looking away before it became uncomfortable. "You seem to be an avid reader," she commented, glancing at the journal he was reading.

"Call it compulsive," he answered and got back to reading.

"On what topics, if I may ask?"

"That depends on what suits my mood or is handy."

"Ah! And I am just the opposite," she said, rolling her eyes. "I mean I am not an avid reader, more of a teenage gossip lover." She smiled, pleased with her joke.

Nikhil glared at her through narrowed eyes. "So what brings you here then, some assignment?" he snapped.

"Nothing really…nothing on my to-do list. Something seemed to draw me here and it certainly wasn't a quest for knowledge," she quipped. "I hope my presence is not disturbing you in any way." He looked at her quizzically, saying nothing. "Don't worry, just take a friend's friend as your friend," she added softly.

"That is always the case — a friend's friend is always welcome." He inhaled sharply, preparing himself for the long conversation he knew was to follow. "When you came, the only thought that crossed my mind was that you wanted to talk about our relationship, because you know about that. It set me off for a minute."

"That is surely something interesting to talk about and fortunately I am the only person who knows." She rested her hands on the table. "It is more interesting that way," she murmured, giving him a crooked grin.

Hating the use of 'interesting' to describe our relationship, he stared back at her. Her sincere, beautiful eyes forced a smile on his face and he said softly, "Could be 'interesting' for you to learn, ponder and talk about, but it's very different for us, it holds a different meaning and value, not meant for gossip."

This quiet assertion surprised her. She tilted her head to one side, gave a cool smile and said, "I didn't mean that."

"I'm sorry, I shouldn't have taken off. I hope you understand that it gets too difficult to justifying oneself in a conventional world," he said, taking a deep breath, feeling edgy and uncomfortable.

"No issues, it just proves your point that this relationship is special. And don't worry, take me as a friend." She paused, fidgeting with the ring on her finger before adding, "And my views shouldn't matter." He nodded in silent acceptance, her friendship and her views.

"Hey, so tell me about the most joyful moment you have had with Anu," she said, trying to make the strained conversation more warm and relaxed.

"That is a difficult question," he murmured, running a

hand over his hair and smiling at Dhriti. As the hands of the clock marked the next hour, he said, "We all seek friendship. It's all about emotions and gaining that human connection – a metaphysical rather than a physical construct. We don't spend time seeking validation for our sexuality; we spend time together because we value the other's presence and wish to grow into the relationship. That makes every moment spent together joyful."

"I know Anuj would express a lot more to you than he would ever say to us."

"But you can't ignore human sexuality. We find solace in each other's company, which allows us to identify ourselves, and that shapes the unique dynamic we have. But it is not everything. A lot more makes this relationship. Well I, for instance, do not have to pretend to be other than who I am, when I am with him, and vice versa." He paused, nostalgia evident on his face as various thoughts crossed his mind. "You know I have felt a lot of ambivalence regarding my own sexuality, often debating with myself, but I could not change. In Anuj's company I can run the gamut from 'I am queer' to 'I am this but I have someone who loves me this way'. This is what he has offered me and vice-versa."

Dhriti was all ears. Mr. Reticent was in form. Dhriti listened as patiently as a catholic priest in confessional.

He paused, trying to gauge her thoughts. "You don't approve of this relationship?" he asked softly.

"I am nobody to approve or not," she replied cautiously.

"But you do not *approve*." Nikhil stressed the last word

"Well, I just find it strange and unfamiliar. To be truthful, I was taken aback when I saw you two kissing."

"That is to be expected. People cannot understand that human hearts and psyche do not always follow established norms." She nodded in agreement. "Well not just because I am living one such relationship, but as an individual I believe that such things should be left to people rather than to societal norms to define them. I hope you understand my stand; love between the same sex creates rhetoric, pain and confusion, but ultimately it is the decision of those involved, to live their lives that way. Sadly, it is always overshadowed by interpretations, some biblical, some societal, some even rational, for it challenges the accepted norms."

Dhriti once again nodded in acceptance. What an intellectual mind this guy was, a thinking man!

"I know the same thoughts must have come to you, but all men are not shaded in the same way; they never can be. It is all about your way of looking at life, at people, deciphering as things change and evolve, doing a meta-synthesis of thoughts, ideas and experiences to find meaning. And this shapes your perceptions and understanding of things; it expands or shrinks the different frames you craft in your mind."

"I don't know… could be my frames are not letting me get the right picture, but for me, it's how I want to view things," Dhriti responded.

"That's fair. No one is stopping you doing that. You may choose to see through your lens rather than mine, but just once, why not try my point of view? Maybe it will help you understand my pain."

"So you say I just need to view the episode differently."

"You have already done that. Frankly, it's your choice. But if your ideas hurt others, can they be right?" he asked, putting aside the journal which had been lying unread all this time.

"He is happy with you. When I realized he was gay, I was shocked, but then I thought that it is his life and he should have the choice to decide how to live it." Dhriti gave her rare smile.

"Yes, but in the matter of choice, he is genetically designed to think independently. He won't change because you want him to," Nikhil warned.

"Hey, I should be leaving. You came here to read. I just happened to see you and took the opportunity to have a talk," she explained.

"It was a pleasure. You are Anu's friend, and hopefully, now mine as well."

"It was great meeting you. You are a gem of a person and you will keep him happy, I know." Her eyes sparkled and Nikhil could not help but smile on hearing this.

"Thanks for the appreciation and I'm honoured," he gently teased.

"Cool. I think I should head back now. We could meet at dinner some time," she said politely.

"I will certainly try to be there about the same time. *Chalo,* I'll get back to my reading."

Once she left, Nikhil informed me about the unprecedented conversation. I was glad.

*****

11

ᵀHE BIG NEWS

Dhriti had promised not to tell Aarya about my relationship. But she assured me, "Even if you opened up, he would not think it wrong." I too, was sure he would stand by me, but I was worried about others knowing. "Are you afraid of facing the truth or worried about what people will say?" Nikhil often asked me. I had no answer. God had not given me such lightness of heart. With wild eyes, I often scanned my surroundings to gauge the expressions of people around us. At times my wide-eyed stare looked accusatory, at other times merely lost.

"Yes I worry," I once answered Nikhil.

"You should not," he murmured in an effort to reassure me. But fear stalked my soul. After that episode with Dhriti, I had become cautious: no kisses in the open, no love-making in random places; locked rooms for all intimate action.

"We could go to my house and make love in my bed," I said one day, as we lay in the afterglow of our love-making.

"Are you nuts?" he asked, rolling his eyes.

"What's the matter? You know the house is empty during the day."

"Maybe…but…" he stammered.

"There wouldn't be anyone there," I said, planting a soft kiss on his lips. "I don't want to wait till your or my room-mate goes out, so we can meet."

"Anu, it isn't as easy as you make it sound. If any of your family member comes to know, it will spell horror for you."

"I said when there is no one at home, which is usually the case. Anyway, it's all up to you. I'm happy as long as you are with me."

"I will keep that in mind," he said with his usual easy smile.

"I want my room to have memories," I said, looking into his dark, humour-filled eyes.

"Good choice," he murmured against my face.

"So should we plan it for this Saturday?" I asked, excited at the thought.

"I accept," he said quietly.

***

Saturday arrived none too soon for me. There was no one at home when we arrived, giving us time and space to be together. I took Nikhil to my room and showed him my things.

"You have a mouth-organ. Can you play?" he asked.

I nodded taking the ancient mouth-organ from him. Raising it to my mouth I began to play my favourite songs. He sat on my bed resting against the wall. *I am for him* repeated like a mantra in my head as I played for him.

"So you hide things from me," he whispered in my ear.

"Not hide; we just never talked about it," I answered.

"You're good, but I've never seen you play in college."

"Since the time we met I have been preoccupied with loving you; that's my full time passion now," I said cheekily.

"Is that so?" he asked, smiling eyes fixed on me. You just couldn't beat him at the game of seduction. "And yet, you still appear to be wearing clothes," he chuckled. "You are making me do the dirty job again," he said, slowly taking off my t-shirt.

My bare body glistened as he moved his nose over my chest then deliberately sucked my nipple. A frisson of excitement ran through me. "You make me feel vile things," I chuckled.

"Oh yes!" he responded, "But you invited me here remember." He touched my lips with his finger.

"Have you ever been so close to anyone in your life?" I asked.

"Not for a long time and never so close as to think about spending our lives together," he responded.

I had always admired his honest answers. "You want us to spend our lives together?" I was so pleased to hear that.

"You have doubts?"

He pressed his tongue against mine and sucked hard. I was being pulled into the gravity of his love and moaned with pleasure. "I love you," he whispered. "And...don't you have plans to take a bath with me?" His eyes glowed with excitement as he rubbed his nose against mine.

Bathing together had been on my bucket list – his touch, gentle soapiness, running water…

"I shall count that in your list of misdemeanours," he warned with a grin.

"Your list is getting a little longer than usual today," I responded. I leaned over and planted a feather soft kiss on his lips. Casually sliding my hands under his T-shirt, I took it off.

"You are slowly learning the rules of the game," he murmured. "You should listen to me more; I am going to be your husband."

The ground seemed to move beneath my feet and my mouth twisted into a triumphant smile. "Indian law doesn't allow us to get married."

"I don't want the court in my bedroom – that's reserved for you and me. I will marry you when I return from Sierra Leone. I'm going there for my internship and first job" he said, as if mentioning an everyday fact.

I was shocked and speechless.

"Things got finalized a week ago. I didn't tell you because I knew you would not like it. Allow me to choose my career path and have faith that I shall come back to you. I don't wanna stay there forever, but I've always wanted to take up war journalism, and fortunately I am getting that chance. A British human rights magazine is hiring me."

I sat looking at him helplessly, refusing to cry. Finally my heart slowed its crazy rhythm and my breathing returned to normal. I was happy for him; he was getting what he wanted.

"Hey Anu, it's only for six months. By then you'll be done with your studies too and we can live together."

I heard him but the words sounded like a death knell, a cruel twist to life. How would I go through the days?

"Hey, don't look at me like that! You know I've always wanted to do this," he said, clasping my face with both hands. "Hey c'mon now, won't you take bath with me?"

"In a while," I said quietly. "Let me make some coffee first."

I picked up my discarded T-shirt and headed towards the kitchen. He followed. Slipping his fingers into the waistband of my jeans, he pulled me back with unexpected audacity, saying, "Let me." My lips pursed. "Sure…that saves some labour," I said, handing him the coffee mugs.

I watched him from a distance. With easy grace he applied butter to bread while the water boiled. I went into the living room and switched on the TV. After some time, he returned to sit beside me on the couch, coffee mugs and buttered bread on on a tray.

"Are you angry?" he asked.

"No, I'm not. I just fear losing you," I said honestly.

"Think about it. If you feel I should stay back, say it; I will. It's just an internship, I can do that anywhere. I can take up similar in India. But do consider this is global exposure I will miss if I stay. And Sierra Leone is a safe country."

I should have been happy but I could not get over the feeling of shock. I told myself it was just for six months, and would kick start his career. That was more important than being together. I stared at him, confused and lost, debating with myself.

"Do you have any idea what you mean to me?"

His words did what they always did, they quickened my pulse. I moaned as he kissed me, realizing that very soon I would lose him and be on my own again. I chose to say nothing but my eyes were moist.

"Coffee?" he said, to distract me.

I nodded, taking a sip. The next instant I had clasped his face with one hand and kissed him. Leaning over me he took the cup from my other hand put it on the table, followed by his own. I slid down to the edge of the sofa. In one fluid movement he placed his knees between my thighs and was over me. I closed my eyes, offering myself completely to him.

"Can you live without me?" he asked.

What a stupid question to break such a magical spell.

"Sure I can, but I wanna live with you," I responded in a low voice.

He smiled, out-smarted by my reply. Gently he curled his hand behind my neck and slid my leg over his, almost lying on me. My breathing became ragged as hot excitement coursed through unexplored parts of my body. I wanted to cross over to the dark side of my psyche, a playground for my desires.

"You're blushing," he murmured, "Why is that?"

"I like it with you."

He closed his eyes and hugged me. "I know. But now, how about some lunch?"

"Let's order…I want to stay in, as we are. This evening you will have to get back to college while I stay here."

"I hope 'evening' means after dinner? Don't worry, I'm a friend and I'm a guy. No one will think anything," he smirked.

I wasn't worried about that either.

***

My sister, coming home at noon, was the first to meet Nikhil. In fact, she came before our lunch order arrived. And Nikhil, with his polished ways, took just minutes to impress her. She talked at length about his plans to go to Sierra Leone and he learnt about her spiritual paths. She spoke to him extensively about his psyche. At times, he looked at me as if to say, '*Now I know where your philosophical roots lie.*'

"You have a gentle heart; you can't hurt anybody," my sister declared.

"What do you say, Anu? Do you think I'm that innocent?" Nikhil asked.

"How can I say? But if Didi says it is so, it must be. I believe her."

"And you will study life in Sierra Leone and find meaning there as well. Behind everything that happens in life, every emotion, there is a reason," Didi told him, only to be interrupted by the doorbell.

"And right now let's find delight in the food which has hopefully arrived," Nikhil said, walking over to open the door.

The food had indeed arrived. We ate while Nikhil and Didi shared some more thoughts and ideas, talking as if they had known each other for years. After lunch, I fell asleep on the sofa, lulled by their voices.

***

Nikhil was to leave the next day for Sierra Leone. Most of his batchmates, including his roomie, had already left for their respective internships. It was easy for me to visit him in his room and spend time together. At times I skipped classes to be with him, telling myself everyone did so in the second year. The fact was I wanted to be with him, refusing to let the thought into my head that I would miss him desperately. He was happy to be leaving to fulfill his dreams. And so life kept moving on...

It was the last day we had made love... After a shower I went straight to Nikhil's room wearing the T-shirt he had bought me, which he called *black desire*. His packing was almost done. He was sitting on his bed in a blue tracksuit, listening to the radio, his hair shampooed. Hearing my hello his mouth twisted into a smile. Putting aside his breakfast plate, he sauntered casually towards me. "I was hoping to see you," he murmured in a sensuous voice.

"I had to," I whispered. I looked at him, trying to hide my fear. He wrapped me in his arms.

The door was open and anyone could have come and caught us, but we were oblivious to these thoughts. He planted a feather soft kiss on my lips before wandering over to the door and locking it. Coming to me, he wiped the tears from my eyes and sat me gently on the bed.

"I will be alone," I said, a hand squeezing my heart.

He looked at me passively, not moving, not saying anything. For a moment we were frozen in the anguish of separation. Tears filled the hazel eyes that had never failed to mesmerize me. Holding each other close, our tears mingling like the water of two holy rivers, carrying our love, loss and despair.

"Are you gonna say goodbye with tears in your eyes?" His voice was a whisper emanating from the depths of his psyche.

I reached across and touched his cheek. His expression softened, vaguely amused at the meaninglessness of my life without him.

"I did not want to cry but you were the one to get emotional first," I said on a shuddering breath.

He smiled. "My fault; I accept."

"Apology accepted but you will have to give me some time to get back to my senses," I murmured.

He kissed me long and hard and then said, "Who can spare that much time?"

Desire rushed through my bloodstream. He would be gone for six months and I would be left alone, wanting and longing.

His hands dropped to my waist. "Now do as you are told," he ordered. "Wrap your legs around mine. Fill me with so much love that I will have enough to last me for the next six months."

I moved as he directed. At times he hit and pinched me, getting raw and aggressive; but I loved it all.

He gazed down at me. "I will come back for you," he promised, slowing sinking into me.

I moaned, flickering like a flame that crackled as it burned bright. The feeling was so exquisite. *There was fullness in the act.* His eyes burned into mine. The want I saw there made me light up inside. I revelled in glory as he pleased me and teased me, bringing us together – forever. Finally he rolled onto his side, gazing down at me as we lay side by side. He sent a feather soft kiss towards me.

"Sex is such a beautiful thing," I murmured, sliding my hand over his waist.

"It is beautiful because you are so damn special. So, what are you going to do while I'm away?"

"Wait for you." The words seem to spill from my mouth of their own accord. "And what about you?" I asked.

"Honestly, I'm still trying to figure that out. I've got used to your tricks and innocuous childish ways. I don't know if I'll be able to hold myself there for six long months." He bent and planted a soft kiss on my lips.

***

It felt like the worst morning of my life. I had lost all desire and reason to get out of bed and welcome the new morn. I failed to let the soft rays of the September sun kiss my body. Nikhil had left last night. We had been together the whole day – tea, dosa, kisses, love-making — everything wove together so beautifully. And then the thread broke and the pearls scattered on the floor. Nikhil — the brief encounter, the moment of connection, the light that flashed so brightly, was gone as quickly as it had come. Time seemed to have moved forward a decade. Yesterday seemed to have happened years ago. It wasn't just sex between us; it was a pure, sacred love.

"You seem to have no energy today," Aarya commented.

"Yeah, just feeling lazy," I replied. That was the best I could think of. "….a bit lost too. Anyways, you need to dress to get to class on time. Are you using the bathroom or can I?"

"You can, I'm already half done," he said, flicking me a quick look.

As I moved towards the bathroom I heard him call, "Hey Anu! You don't have to hide things from me… I know. I figured it out some time ago. So don't worry, you can open up anytime you want."

I nodded, trying to smile. How foolish I had been to think he knew nothing, that I had hidden my feelings so cleverly!

"And we haven't have had a whisky session for a long time… perhaps this evening?" The smile on his face seemed to say: *Don't worry, bro, I am here for you.*

Aarya had known my truth all this time but had never revealed that — no action, no reaction. He was stolid, stoic and true. He knew I was struggling to hold onto the golden grains of sand as they ran through my fingers.

"You need to hurry or we'll be late for class," he yelled as I sauntered towards the bathroom.

***

We got down to practicing our evening religion again – drinking. It has been quite some time since we had had a drink together. Aarya had made extra preparations and we had stir-fried chicken, noodles and chilled beer. Aarya sat leaning against the bed, his long legs stretched out in front of him. I sat cross-legged beside him, rather like a schoolboy who feared a lecture. The Backstreet Boys crooned softly in the background.

"That's good," Aarya commented appreciatively as he offered me some chicken and then dug into his own food, eating like he had been on a fast. "Sorry I'm strapped for cash, so we have to settle for beer," he said apologetically.

"No issues. We can maintain a liquor fund and pledge to deposit ten rupees a day for emergency requirements," I suggested.

He nodded, buying the idea. "This will do fine for now though," he commented as he poured the beer and then raised his mug. "To our friendship!" he said slowly and clearly. "Now, would you like to say something?"

"What should I say? You know everything; you said you had figured it out." My lips quirked upwards into a half-smile

"Not just me, I believe everyone has. It was so evident – you two would be together for hours, take long night walks, give each other intense looks and smiles. It wasn't hard to come to the right conclusion. I didn't ask but it was evident."

"I always feared that," I murmured.

"He did too," Aarya said matter-of-factly. "Nikhil had a talk with Dhriti and me before leaving. He was considering not going to Sierra Leone. He was concerned about you. He's a good guy, I must say."

I stared at him dumbfounded. When I got my voice back I asked curiously, "Didn't you feel bad to have a gay roomie?"

"I think I was the first one to know. Your face is so transparent and honest. I know you look at me when I change. At first I felt bad about it. Then with your thing with Nikhil — I felt odd, really odd. For a while I was completely pissed off and even applied for a room change. Since I did not give a reason I was refused. You have always been good to me so I did not want to bring this thing out into the open."

"We could have had a talk," I said, alarm bells jangling in my head.

"There was no opportunity, but I realized we could still be friends. I had a word with Dhriti; she had not seen you guys kissing then. She was shocked and did not want to believe it. She has always had a soft corner for you, boy. When I look back I feel I was wrong to want to change rooms. If I had left, you would have been in a weaker position."

I said staring at the floor, unable to make eye contact. "He has possessed me so wholly that I can think of nothing but him. He is intoxicating. I am caught in his net, unable to move, unwilling to free myself. It didn't take me long to realize that all I want throughout my life is this."

"Well it happens. You know, after all this I've come to realize that though we are different, at the same time we are similar. I once wanted to run out on you but now I feel that your loving Nikhil is the same as my loving Dhriti."

I made another drink for him. I smiled as he talked; we were talking after such a long time, actually talking. For months I had not given any attention to his love story. I realized that in the wake of having one thing around, I had unintentionally kept many things away. As we talked, I gradually felt liberated from the charmed trap. Aarya never showered me with sympathy; he was supportive and understanding, things I had never seen in him before. We all evolve with changing situations, with the tides of time. Without our knowing it, our friendship had evolved into something deeper.

"I will say one thing though," he said, nodding his head wisely. "Our society still lives in the 19th century. We have definitions of what is normal and what is queer and we are not prepared to accept the latter. Anu, you are queer for people but right for yourself. Brace yourself to face the hidden fear of society for what they consider queer. Today they say things behind your back; tomorrow they will abuse you to your face. Nikhil feared that would happen, and I fear it too. But it is you who has to live through it.

He was voicing the thoughts I had chosen to set aside. "I know," I mumbled, sipping my beer.

"Never forget we are with you. You've always been a good friend," Aarya said, savouring his chicken and lifting my sullen mood with his words.

Once done, we washed our hands, switched off the lights and got into bed. The moon was up and silver light flooded the room. I gazed out at the stars wondering why Aarya had never reacted, even after knowing the truth. I knew he would not tell me what exactly he felt and had an uncanny ability to evade anything that seemed inappropriate to him. He had tried that on me several times, discussing only the things he wanted to. Either way, I was relieved I had people who would stand by me under any circumstance.

*****

Time flew by. I barely realized that two months had passed. Some things had got worse while others had shaped up nicely. Nikhil and I did not talk much, most of our communication being limited to e-mails, though he did call me at few times from his office. Aarya and Dhirti were supportive and things were going well between them.

"We are planning to get married after the course ends, assuming we can get decent jobs to fend for ourselves," Dhriti told me.

"Cool! That means I'll have feasts on both sides," I replied.

"Anu, you have the job of welcoming the guests from the bride's side!"

"But Dhriti, you know Aarya is *my* best friend!"

"That is why I'm asking him to take the responsibility of welcoming the guests. I know no one will be able to do it better than you. I want our marriage to be remembered as a union of three souls."

She left me speechless. I could only smile and nod, foolishly pleased, leaving the matter to be finally settled between bride and groom.

My college mates, if unsure, had noticed ample indications about my sexual orientation. Though no one was upfront about it, I sometimes overheard them talking about me. I had become gossip material; I had been for a long time. Nikhil and I had had almost a year-long intense relationship. It remained hidden initially on the pretext of tennis and because society assumes things to be straight. Two guys can have a deep friendship. But in time, the intensity of our friendship began to be questioned. When one is different, one tends to turn stolid. That is the story of change-makers, of rebellions, and that was our story too. We built a cocoon, knowing we had a safe haven in each other. We gave little thought to what others said.

Things had changed somewhat in Nihkil's absence. I had no one to surrender myself to. At times I wept in the dark; at times it became difficult to face those who stared at me, disdain in their eyes. They did not speak, just stared – their dark eyes questioning, blaming, sometimes abusive. I kept my gaze low lest my eyes meet theirs. At times I felt like running away to a place where nobody knew me, where I would not have to face those questioning looks. But there was no such place. I had all reason to weep and I had all reason to smile.

"Don't worry, he will come back," Aarya would say to console me. "And he is not the only one who cares for you. We love you too."

"You can't understand how I feel when I see others flaunting their love, thinking about marriage. I just can't do that; I can't have that life."

"I know it is easier for us, people accept the norm, but do you always need people's acceptance?"

"Easy to say man, hard to implement."

"Hey buddy, don't be so downcast. I shall always be there, standing by you. People will forget my love story, but they will remember yours," he grinned. "Just be happy. Remember you have to do all our assignments or else all three of us will fail!"

"Ah, so you are my friend so I can do all your assignments?"

"Also for our assignments," he responded playfully.

"You always try to console me; what makes you think I'm so sad?" I asked, my voice low.

"I would be most happy if you proved me wrong" he retorted. Blinking his eyes he asked quietly, "Do you fear something?"

His words hit me like a wrecking ball. "I fear who I am. I don't *want* to be this. I hate feeling ignored because of who I am. I feel aggrieved by what people think about me. I fear how people treat me, see me, talk about me. It is wearying and unpalatable."

"Anu, I can't be in your shoes but I can say that you must either live the way *you* want, or the way others want you to. The third option is live as they want you to but in your own way," he said, his voice concerned.

"I didn't understand the third option."

"Live the way people expect but what happens behind closed doors concerns you only. No one can put up a 'I want information' placard outside your bedroom. You understand what I am saying? You must be perceived to live a normal life. People don't accept your relationship, neither does the Indian law. I know it is about emotions, but let it remain a hidden dynamic. Let it remain hidden. Strip yourself of these chains of fear and guilt; the world can be a dark place." Aarya's face wore an uncharacteristically serious expression.

I just listened, thinking 'what he says is right'. Finally I asked the question uppermost in my mind. "Aarya, how can I hide something that is already in the open? People know about it. Everyone in the college knows. Perhaps my parents will also know soon...what then?"

He nodded soberly. "People love to gossip. Yes, they will talk about it, but eventually they will choose to forget and move on. No one cares for old news."

Not that I was afraid of people; I just did not want to face them.

A few days later, I received a call from Nikhil. He said he was enjoying his work, the culture; he was concerned about the sorry state of democracy there, the restrictions imposed on the media, the internal strife. It was all soul-soup for him. It was what he wanted to do. We talked for a long time. He inquired about Aarya and Dhriti. For a moment the four of us seemed like a family, sharing deep emotions, ready to hold hands and walk together in search of happiness. We talked of happy times. He sounded content; he was doing what made him feel like an achiever. He knew what he wanted from life and he had gone after it.

*****

12

THE GUILT DEEPENS

I had no intention of doing what I did that day. I had not planned it nor prepared my answers. It just happened.

"Is something wrong?" my sister asked, concerned by my uncharacteristically quiet demeanour.

"Just study pressure," I muttered.

"Something emotional perhaps?" she asked gruffly. It was not easy to pull the wool over her eyes.

"Why are you asking this?" The lump at the back of my throat burned with suppressed tears.

"I know something is wrong," she said softly.

"But you are wrong this time."

"And I fear, as usual, that I am not. There is something you are hiding; I can see it in your eyes. You can't lie to me."

"I'm fine really, Di."

She leaned back, studying me intently. "If you say so… I was just a bit worried," she said slowly, a bittersweet smile on her face. She sighed deeply and said, "You left your email open and I happened to glance at a mail which gave me the idea you are emotionally attached to someone. Seeing you so upset I was merely drawing the correct conclusions."

I flushed, feeling uncomfortable. "Is that all?" I asked, wondering how much she in fact knew. If she had read any of my mails to Nikhil, she would know.

"Hmm…but some things require an explanation," she said.

"I request you to leave it; there is nothing flippant about the whole matter, I can assure you." I couldn't hide my exasperation and my voice was cold and hard.

"I said some things demand an explanation," she snarled.

I glanced nervously at her. Her steeliness seemed to indicate she knew; she had just been waiting for the right time to confront me I concluded. In that moment she looked utterly hostile – a sister I had never known.

"Well, are you…attached to someone?" she snapped.

I picked up my jacket and stood up. Turning to her I said as quietly as my hammering heart would allow, "I am in a relationship with a guy, Di. I am gay."

The words I had so feared were out. All my worst fears, packaged into that one short sentence, were released from their bindings. Di had been more than a mother to me. There was no hiding my living truth.

"Anuj!" she gasped.

Tears filled my eyes as I gazed at her. She stared back, amazed.

"If *you* decide not to support me, I cannot expect to receive it from anyone," I said, fear of rejection raw in my voice.

"How is this possible? Who else knows?"

"Some of my close friends; but I fear others have figured it out," I replied, some unnamed, dark emotion flooding my heart.

She bit her lip, looking up at the ceiling, her eyes wet.

"I should have told you," I said softly.

"I can understand why you could not. I don't really know how to react."

"As you would to anyone else if I was not your brother."

"I wouldn't have cared then," she replied quietly.

"So you care only because I am your brother?"

"It's not that Anu, it's about how people will view it."

"Do you consider it wrong?" I asked.

"Anything that is not considered normal is taken to be wrong," she answered dryly.

I looked at her, feeling my strongest support in the world shaken. I regretted telling her but then she would have had to know someday.

***

"I think she knew or had guessed after reading one of my emails. I thought it better to tell her the truth." I was feeling wistful and maudlin again.

Dhriti, who had been listening patiently for the last half hour, responded to say, "How has she been behaving to you?"

"I know she cares for me and will accept me, but her eyes ask for a thousand apologies."

She nodded her face expressionless. "Weren't you prepared for that?" she asked.

"It still hurts. I am not wrong Dhriti. I cannot change who I am. The only choices I have are to disregard my feelings or live a dual life."

"That's even worse. If you cannot be who you are, what's the purpose in living at all?"

"Thanks for understanding. Most people do not."

"Many people will," she assured me. "It is *your* life and nobody else has any business in it. It's just that you assume people will take it in the wrong way; in fact, they may have thoughts and ideas or they may not care. After all, your existence does not harm them. In a talk I had with my cousin, I got to know that he harbours thoughts for a guy friend though he is dating a girl he is drawn to. He is attracted to both sexes but cannot say so; people would consider it wrong or see him as a sex-addict. He wouldn't have said any of this had I not narrated your story. People around us have stories but they just do not come out." Dhriti's voice was soft but scornful. "I too, held a contrary view when I came upon you two. Things changed for me when I had a talk with you, and then Nikhil. Everyone has a right to live the way they want," she said firmly.

I smiled. She had been such a support. Everyone should have such a friend. But I knew that not everyone would think like her. I would have to endure doubt and the most excruciating confrontations. While part of me was glad I had been open, another part of me was sad and weary having faced so much in such a short time. I gave myself a mental shake. They had been moments of reality, of self- realization in answer to 'who am I?' and 'what do I want?' There were bigger hows and whys waiting to be confronted. Truths would be revealed. I closed my eyes for a moment, as if to hold back the inevitable. Nikhil was my partner in moving from darkness to light. We had to guide each other; we had to lay our ghosts.

"If ever my story is told, it would resonate with the tale of our friendship rather than my love," I said, my mouth twisting in amusement.

"We are an extended family. I want you to know that I care for you and always will," Dhriti murmured.

I remembered Aarya telling me she had always had a soft corner for me. Cool! I gave her a sardonic smile.

"It's been quite a day," she said. Recently we had turned emotional consultants for each other.

"With you, every day is quite a day," I said.

She smiled, her eyes trying to find her old bubbly friend in this person lost in the dreary present.

The fireball in the sky was making way for the moon. Myriad shades bathed us in evening glow. The lights of the hostel had been turned on; they appeared like soft beacons in the gathering dusk.

"So which is the most romantic place you have ever been to?" Dhriti asked suddenly.

The question made me laugh, or rather, the thought of the answer did. She gave me a 'what's the matter, dude?' look.

"When I ask Nikhil out on a date, the only thing that comes to his mind is dosa!"

Now we both were laughing. But Dhriti was nothing if not persistant. "But you still have not answered my question: Which is the most romantic place you two have been to?" she reiterated.

"Oof…that's difficult!" I let out a deep breath and said, "I think, when you saw us that day. We had had a big fight and gone out to make up. You were witness to that."

"You know, your love story gives my imagination wings, it's incredibly lovely!"

I laughed self-consciously, looking up at the dying colours of the sky. My gaze came back to her face as I asked, "But you didn't tell me what was yours."

'Mine? For me, the first kiss was memorable. You know, after that I questioned myself for two days whether he was the right person for me."

"And is he?" I asked teasingly.

She looked at me, her eyes big and round, a crafty smile tugging at the corners of her mouth. "Yesss… So, in your case, who propositioned first?" she asked, keenly interested.

'Umm....I did. He seems so unemotional, but somewhere deep down, I got the feeling he liked my company, so I made the first move. It's never easy for a guy to proposition another guy – one can never predict the consequences. In my case, it just worked. It was quite a gamble though!"

"Great that it clicked. Hey man, I want you both at my wedding, as a couple – a very cute couple!" she said.

I gave her a half-hug, whispering, "I love you." It is hard to find love and harder still to find a true friend. I blinked momentarily. I had not felt so alive, so vital since Nikhil left. That evening with Dhriti, everything seemed black or white; there were no greys in my life. I found the support I had so desired. There were no opinions about living dual lives, no talk of having shamed the family, no guilt in eyes, no 'I say this because I care for you'; just honest friendship. It is amazing that a simple walk and an hour's talk can make life seem richly coloured again.

I was learning more about myself than at any time before. I am not a weak person; I was not then either. I had been prepared to face everything in order to soar high like Icarus, flying close to sun, without a thought to getting melted. I had nothing to lose when I was flying with Nikhil. Being with him had been an education for me. I learnt about my body, my limits, my desires, my tolerance, my innocence and my love.

When I was a child I believed there was a clock in my heart, with little hands which marked time. I wish someone had told me those hands could easily be broken and good times changed in a jiffy to bad. I would then never have believed the clock fuelled life, and been more open to change, more ready for uncertainties, more prepared for crashes. I wish someone had told me never to wait for the hour of fortune.

Time seemed to have taken a sharp turn; two years of college was nearing their end. This meant Nikhil would be returning in a few days. Though he had wanted to stay on, he was returning for me. I chuckled thinking about it; I felt special. I had learnt to live the reality. My learning curve had been sharp. The Icarus in me once again soared high towards the sun, without thought or fear. I had entered an alternate universe.

***

"Are you upset with me?" I asked my sister.

"Why would I be?" she murmured, her voice stiff.

"You are misunderstanding me."

"I cannot, by virtue of the bond we share…but many people will." She took a deep breath and then added, "They form the majority."

"So you are worried about me?" I asked, my mouth dry.

"This is the only thing I can do now."

"You can do a lot better if you wish. Support me, stand by me; protect me." My childish need eclipsed more mature emotions. I looked to her as a child looks to his mother for approval.

Her eyes spoke of anxiety, her expression of unwillingness, but her heart retained all the fond memories of moments we had shared. She regarded me with alarm. I knew that for my parents it would be difficult to acknowledge my relationship. I needed her support.

She did not move, her gaze fixed on me, her expressions changing from helplessness to insecurity. "Are you thinking of opening up to mom and dad?" she asked.

"I've not thought about it.'"

"Do you think it can remain hidden from them?"

"No…some day they will know. I will have to open up," I answered dryly.

"That will be a difficult day."

"Who will you stand by on that day?"

"I am reluctant to stand by either side," she said, her expression cautious. Closing her eyes, she fell into deep, brooding silence.

"You'll leave…" I said sadly.

"Do you think so little of me?" she asked in a heavy voice. "We know so little about each other or we are so set up in our own esteem that we belittle the other's emotions," she said, her voice mournful.

I sat up. "Do you think so?"

"Anuj, my problem is that I can neither be happy for you nor go against you. But I will be with you, for us."

"Thanks!" A heavy load lifted from my heart.

"Now relax. Don't think so much; things won't change. I will be better employed making coffee for us instead of talking." She rolled her eyes at the wall clock.

"I promise to know you better," I said as she sauntered towards the kitchen.

Turning, she replied, "I thought you wanted me to know you prefer light coffee. Anything with coffee…toast, biscuits?"

"A good cheese sandwich."

"Cheesy honey!" she teased, her mouth twisting in a smirk.

We shared a laugh, a much needed laugh. I knew Didi would stand by me; when was the only question. It is a great relief to know that things can break but still exist, bound by love. It had been a journey of pain and ecstasy for me, but above all, to know myself and the world around me.

"Here's your cheese sandwich and coffee."

"Thanks! Your coffee will always bring me back to you," I said, my eyes gleaming.

"Why, are you going somewhere?" she asked jokingly.

"I feel distracted."

"I can see that. What is it you want?" she asked, giving me her no-nonsense stare.

"Him."

"If you are so clear, what distracts you? Enlighten me"

"A question: Can we spend our whole lives together?" My words almost fell over each other.

She nodded slowly, her eyes darkening. The implications of what I had said hung between us. Her eyes explored my mind. The idea was threatening…devastating. "In my profession I have come across people who tried homosexuality but then settled down to a normal life, getting married, having kids, retiring. Do you really see this fling as a lifetime commitment?" she asked.

For a moment I felt a fleeting stab of disappointment and anger. "Di, I love him! I know I could never settle down with a girl."

"I too, think I could never settle down with anyone, but then I know I must."

"Di…I am bottom. I am the yin in our act. I am attuned to that role. I cannot be with a girl; I will end up destroying her life." The naked reality of my life seemed to lie before in those words. I took a deep breath.

For a moment she said nothing, her eyes dark, her face jaundiced. She was seeking for the right words, or perhaps strength. Sex is not a hot word in drawing rooms, let alone sex between those of the same gender. They are 'hear and forget' stories, not even fodder for juicy gossip. It is considered a bestial act.

"You are the yin…" she said slowly, each word trembling with shock and disgust.

I couldn't look into her eyes. This time I didn't feel a victim but a culprit. "I have the same traits as you," I said rebelliously, still looking down. I knew she would take time to understand and accept. Understanding is such a fragile thing. I would have to give her time.

"Do you know what it will do to our parents?" she whispered, revulsion clear in her voice.

"I know. That's why I told you and not them. I hoped you would understand. It is not my fault I am this way," I said, my voice low, speaking of my helplessness.

"Give me time," she finally said. I could hear the same helplessness and agony in her voice.

She was both nervous and disturbed. I was struck by the fact that we shared this habit of getting nervous easily. I held my breath, waiting for her response, anxiety building within me. But she did not speak. She sat there expressionless and stolid.

"I love him. I want to be with him," I said gently, breaking the silence.

She lifted her brows, gave me a hard, discomfiting stare. "Then what is the issue?" she asked coldly.

I looked at her, startled by her reply. Did she really not know? "You know how it is Di."

"When *you* know no one will accept this, why on earth are you forcing it on me?"

I had never heard her speak so loudly and rudely. "Because I thought you, the person I rely on the most, would help me tide over those remarks," I said, anger blazing into flame. "Didi, I don't want sympathy, I just want you to understand it is not wrong. There are lakhs of people who live this way without telling anyone…without opening up even to their loved ones. All those people are not wrong, neither have they wronged anyone.

They just chose to live the way they wanted to. It is biological Didi. And frankly, I don't want to live a closet life, at least with the people I love, who matter to me. I want them to accept me."

"Anu, I need time to accept this truth. I don't know if I can understand or not, but I will not cast you off either," she said clearly and then walked towards her room.

Even that much was an achievement for me. She had brought me up, been with me more than my mother. I had always looked to her before taking any decision. How could I not involve her in the biggest decision of my life? She had to know everything. It was something I had to do.

*****

13

⊘NE GOOD HUG

⊘t was seven o'clock and the sun's trudge across the sky had ended. It was a fine evening. The breeze blew softly on my face as I walked the cobbled pathway leading to the Bamboo Grass Café, a small eatery at the college boundary. A bell tingled as one opened the door. Designed in an earthy way, the café spoke of the rural affiliations of the owner. Bamboo thickets and dim lights added to the ambience. The café was a regular haunt for *gupshup*.

I had reached before the appointed time, as usual. I stepped in and went to my usual table. Clouds hung over the horizon. The sky had turned into an artist's palette with myriad hues. The sombre stillness was animated by sudden cracks of lightning. It was a sure sign that the night would bring a downpour. I could almost smell the sodden earth as the hot potatoes baked in the hot ashes of the coal fire. I looked around. A crow sat atop a tree, settling into her cozy nest for the night.

Within minutes it got dark and I was still waiting. Dhriti had never been this late. Far from the lights and bustle of this *gupshup* post, I had chosen a desolate corner. It was dark and silent. Finally I saw Dhriti ambling towards me, smiling. She was late, and I had waited for close to an hour. She sat down and poured me a cup of hot, steaming coffee. Yellow light from a small hanging lamp made a feeble attempt to fill the emptiness. Steam rose from the coffee cups in a resolute effort to transcend the earth and reach the sky.

"Your coffee is getting cold. Why so lost? It's your birthday," she said, breaking the silence.

I absently took a sip. "And that's why I was made to wait and wait?" I snapped

"But I've made sure you won't regret waiting," she commented, a knowing smile playing on her lips.

"So should I expect a big gift?"

"Depends on how you take it – as a gift or a prize," she said, shrugging her shoulders

"I'm expecting something big then. Where is Aarya?"

"He'll join us soon. Let's order something."

"Sure. Why not order some starters?"

"All yours," she said, offering me the menu. When I did not take it, she asked impatiently, "What?"

"Nothing, I'm just anxious to see Aarya," I muttered unconvincingly.

"You're always excited to see guys," she complained.

"Allow me to correct you…only handsome guys."

"You had the smartest guy in college with you. Anyway, I am ordering rolls…if you want something else, tell me."

"Rolls work for me."

She signaled to the waiter and gave him the order.

"Aarya is on his way, right?" I asked again.

Dhriti raised her eyebrows. "What is destined will happen?"

I looked back to see Aarya walking towards our table. "Destiny is a strong word. What has it offered you, my friend?" he asked, tapping me on the shoulder.

"Definitely two great friends," I replied promptly.

"It has offered you one more thing if you care to look back," Aarya whispered in my ear.

To please him I looked back. He was right – my destiny stood there – Nikhil. I was astounded, unable to believe it was really him. Nikhil! I was surprised, enthralled and nervous all at the same time. For a second I didn't move or react.

"Happy Birthday Anu!" Dhriti came forward to hug me. "Hope you loved the surprise gift," she murmured.

I could only smile like an idiot. I looked at Nikhil. He was hardly ten meters from me, smiling, relaxed, his eyes crinkling with boyish charm. I rose and took a step towards him as he closed the distance between us. He hugged me, our foreheads pressed together, my body feeling like jelly.

"I came the day before yesterday but I wanted to give you a surprise, so I got in touch with Dhriti and asked her to arrange this evening for all of us," he said, giving me a wink. His words resonated in my ears and in my heart.

"No explanations needed. I'm so happy!" I said, beaming at them all.

"It'll be our first dinner all together," Aarya remarked.

It was so good to see my closest friends so excited for us. In the last six months my world had seemed to come to a standstill, then tilt and spin on a new axis. But it was behind me now. He had come and I savoured every moment, gazing into his earnest, hazel eyes.

"Anuj, are you ready to raise a toast to the best birthday you ever had?" Aarya asked, a slow smile spreading across his face. I nodded.

"So be it," Nikhil said taking a bottle of wine from his bag. "This is red wine from Sierra Leone. There is nothing worth bringing from that country so I had to make do with this."

"Everything is worth millions today," Dhriti added without hesitation, her voice warm and definite.

I could not stop smiling. I marvelled at how easily this man could make me melt.

"I will have beer if you don't mind," Nikhil announced, popping the chilled can open with practiced ease.

The music of the popping can was gleefully followed by the symphony of the hissing cork from the wine bottle. While we busied ourselves with the drinks, Dhriti ordered a table load of good rustic Indian fare. Nikhil sighed as familiar smells began to wrap around us like a comforting blanket.

"So how was Sierra Leone?" Dhriti wanted to know.

"Good for the purpose I went for. Not so good otherwise," Nikhil answered with his usual precision.

"Where are you putting up?" Aarya asked

"Still searching for a decent place but right now I'm at a hotel in Paharganj. Would prefer something near the office," Nikhil told him before adding, "By the way, it was a well thought out surprise and a good party plan,"

Aarya winked at Dhriti, the party planner. I shared a glance with Nikhil. We all dug into the delicious food. Nikhil, of course, enjoyed the meal the most, having been starved for Indian food for months.

"It seems like years since I ate tandoori rotis," Nikhil said, closing his eyes in bliss. "Even the dal tastes sublime!"

"Anuj told me you believe in a low calorie diet," Dhriti mentioned casually.

"Not today for sure," Nikhil replied, picking up a huge cheese-packed paratha roll.

I smiled at him, his quirky sensuous smile making my inner goddess dance.

Dhriti and Aarya left us after dinner. "My cute man, the surprise was for you, not us. We were here just to give you company," she said, bending to give me a peck on the cheek.

Finally we were alone, after a gap of six months. He fixed his gaze on me, making me feel naked. I squinted affectionately.

"So how are you?" he asked, relaxed.

"Not good."

"I am back, my dear." There was both assurance and reassurance in his voice. I smiled. "Want to go for a walk?"

I nodded, my heart full. "I did not know it was so easy for things to stick around," I said to him.

"You are talking about our relationship." When I nodded, he inclined his head to one side and said in a low voice meant only for me, "I am happy to be back for you."

The cool breeze caressed our bodies, bringing with it high voltage passion. He lifted my chin with two fingers and bent to kiss me. After six months I felt life course through my veins. I wrapped myself around him like a vine.

"I missed you!" he said passionately and kissed me again.

I surrendered myself to the moment. I wished I could pause time, like a little clock in my heart.

***

Nikhil closed the door and gazed at me warily. "Everything okay?" he asked, tilting his head and looking at me with concern. "I asked if everything was okay. What is it? I am back now." His voice sounded young and rejuvenated.

I shook my head. "There's nothing to worry about, you know. Worrying is my favourite pastime. Just leave it."

Nikhil loomed in front of me and grasped my chin. Tipping my head back he looked into my eyes, trying to read my fears.

"I told you it's nothing. I worry about making decisions, sticking to what I want. This is not the time to discuss my confusions," I said, pulling my chin away.

Putting a hand on my waist he pulled me closer. I could smell his fresh, familiar aroma. "Let's take a bath together," he suggested, his mouth twisting into an ingenuous smile.

I had lived this moment in my dreams, longing for our bodies and souls to come together.

"Come," he said, clasping my hand firmly and pulling me towards the spacious bathroom.

I saw myself in the mirror, looking strangely lost. "I told Didi about us," I confessed in a rush.

He blew out a breath. "I won't ask what she said or how she reacted. I haven't come back to know that, so just chill. You told her; good for you." He furrowed his brow at me, as if trying to read my mind. "So is that the reason for not taking interest in me?" he asked.

"But I am," I mumbled. Privately I was puzzled by his reaction to what I had said. He didn't seem to care.

"No you are not," he muttered, pulling me into a warm embrace. He kissed my forehead and reiterated, "No you are not. And I am not used to it. My instinct is telling me to beat the fear out of you, but I feel helpless too. You have always known they would not support you; you were prepared. And yet it still worries you. You do realize you are spoiling this romantic moment?"

He put a finger on my lips and then slowly took off his shirt. His clean shaven chest gleamed. Joy flooded my being. I inched forward into his embrace, never wanting this to end. I had longed for him – his eyes, lips, smile, words and whispers, silence and sighs – I had longed for him.

"Come," he said, releasing me.

I took off my clothes and unbuttoned his. Once again we were locked in an unforgettable embrace. We loved and learned from each other. We had our share of fears and internal demons, but we pushed each other to overcome them. We lived in faith and love.

I followed him into the cascading water, closing my eyes, succumbing to the comforting warmth. He watched the water drop a covering of pearls over my body. His fingers trailed from my nape to my waist, tantalizing me, arousing the pleasure hormones. He continued downward, his lips on my chest, his skilled fingers between my legs. "You need soap," he murmured.

My lids opened in a flurry and I gazed straight into his wet, glorious eyes. They gave nothing away. Lathering his hands, he placed them on me. I took the soap from him and slowly moved from his sternum down to his belly, soaping and rubbing as I went. I stared at him, smiling. He grasped my face and kissed me, the water falling in a torrent. My throat clenched, my heart constricted and my emotions swelled. I felt close to tears. It was unstoppable. At that moment I wanted nothing but for the two of us to stay locked in that embrace under the showerhead forever.

"I was aching for you to trust me," he murmured against my mouth.

I surrendered myself completely to him.

***

It had started to rain outside. The sudden, unwanted shower lashed against the window panes. Dark clouds had overpowered the humble sky. The wind whinnied like a wild horse, running wild in accompaniment to my desire. There was a twinkle in his eye. Brows arched, lips curved, his face quivered with excitement. He was beautiful. I couldn't contain my jubilation. In stunned silence I wondered at my good fortune. I had with me the most beautiful gift of God. I looked at him, thanking the lucky star I was born under. His soft look confessed deep elemental desire as I reached up to clasp his handsome face and kiss him gently, pouring all my love into one sweet organic connection.

"I'm happy you're back. I was alone without you, though Dhriti and Aarya have been great supports to me," I told him, clinging to his naked body, enjoying the drizzle outside.

"You're lucky. I never had such friends."

"You never wanted to share yourself with others. I don't think any of your mates know you."

"That's not so," he replied softly, gazing down at me. "I have tried but I never had good listeners."

I stifled a smile. "Would you like to share now?" I asked.

"You ask wrong questions," he said, pursing his lips. Pulling me to him his mouth closed on mine, coercing my lips apart.

Suddenly he pulled back. "Have I never told you about my past?"

"No," I pouted childishly.

"I had a relationship before with a friend in school… four years ago. He was my first crush – as fresh, childish and innocent as you. I liked him. I knew very well that he harboured gay thoughts."

"Jay, I believe his name was? You have mentioned him but never in detail," I responded.

He ran his fingers through my hair and closed his eyes, as if seeking some divine guidance. "We had a good relationship going. He would often come to my house, sometimes when my parents were out. Our meetings were finely orchestrated. It wasn't hard for people to guess. My mother guessed too."

"Your mother!" I cried, startled and alarmed.

His expression changed. "She wasn't sure though. She had her doubts but wasn't sure. But I wouldn't tell her, knowing she would be shocked," he said, a pained look on his face.

I felt a crushing disappointment. "Where is he now?"

"In Delhi," he said immediately, shaking his head and offering a relaxed smile.

I looked at him – the most sleek person I had ever seen. If his past was in the same city, was he just using me for…? "And so?" I asked in a murmur, my vulnerability like a mist between us.

"I often went to meet him and we made love. He got me to meet people, showed me the secret gay hangouts in the city. I learnt a lot from him. But he did not want a long-term relationship, so we broke up."

"Did this happen before I came into your life?" I asked.

"Well before…I explored options in the first year." He gave me a half smile. "I tried finding options but I wanted a stable relationship, not a hook-up thing. I explored the gay clubs too."

"I had no idea…"

He looked down and wrapped me in a tight hug. "That doesn't surprise me," he said, smiling.

I blinked at him, my face stung with a strawberry flush. "But you never told me all this."

"I did not want my past flings to affect our relationship. You mean more to me than all that," he muttered.

More! The little word hung like a tantalizing vision between us.

"You and I know what we want from each other. I never wanted my past to haunt our present. I have agonized over this more than you. I know what we are. Sometimes that places a great physical and psychological drain upon us. But I have decided my life is only with you and I don't care about anything else." He lay back, done.

My heart was racing like a mad thing. "You would leave everyone and live with me?" I asked, my throat dry.

"I have come back for that. In a couple of years my mother will start discussing marriage proposals with me and our tough times will begin. I don't want to wrong any girl but I know my mother will not understand. It will be hard."

"You will have to open up some time." I wished I could calm the thudding in my chest.

"You were quite the first mover in that weren't you; spanking some shit! I can imagine how your sister must have reacted," he said, inhaling deeply.

"I'd rather think I spanked the shit out of her when I told her she and I had shared traits! But that's not the point. The fact is our relationship will never be accepted. We cannot expect to meet people like Aarya and Dhriti everywhere. They probably understand us as they are unaffected by our relationship. Our families will be different."

He gave me an amused smile, somehow bringing back my lost composure. His smile was like a powerful tonic, it gave me strength to face situations.

"Don't worry. We'll figure it out when those problems come," he said in a low voice, running a finger along my jaw.

His touch resonated deep within me, sending delicious tingles down my spine.

***

Things moved on. I had six more months to do in college before taking up an internship and then a job. I needed Nikhil to help me start my career. Ironically, he had got placed in an advertising firm, contrary to anything he had done before or wished to do. It's a strange thing, life, but its very strangeness makes it enticing.

I knew Niks was not the type of guy who would settle down with whatever came onto his plate, he would move on and find his niche.

It happened when we were out watching a soccer match. It brought back memories of Harshit which I had shielded myself from. Niks had become interested in the game while he was in Africa.

"Every evening you can find kids playing football on the dusty streets," he recalled. "I know nothing about the game," I told him, secretly happy to be dragged along.

"Nor I," he retorted, to my surprise. "But it'll be enjoyable. And the best part is one of the teams has never won a match."

"Where do you get these statistics from? I don't see anyone on the ground who could have told you that," I said, scanning the almost empty stadium.

"You underestimate the game. In Africa it is celebrated as a sacred rite, the worship of man's grit and ambition; it is a game the gods play, it is like a battle, a show of action, passion, tenacity and endurance. But above all, it is a way of overcoming fear and knowing oneself. People celebrate it in every street, every evening, talk about it over tea at formal and casual meets. For them soccer is the harshness and sweetness of life disguised as a game, celebrated with trophies and tears, with backroom humour and spectator participation."

Soccer was a completely different affair on the ground than on the idiot box. Contrary to my wild imaginings, there was no stream of young fans arriving with banners streaming colour, dressed in dazzling hues, to witness this war of the gods. There was no hubbub. I waited in vain for the stadium to fill. We were the only ones. But my boy was engrossed in the game from the moment the spherical object was placed in the middle of the ground. I sat brooding on this impossibly wrong application of the word 'excitement'.

My helpless mystification was broken by an occasional roar from the players on the ground, celebrating like a pride of lions that had spotted its lunch. Almost half the match had passed and I still had not figured out the two teams. Nikhil did tell me but his dramatic explanation had somehow not penetrated into my brain. Absorbed in the gladiatorial spirit of the twenty odd men on the field, he didn't notice me snoozing. Finding myself totally neglected I closed my eyes.

"You prefer something else, huh?" Glancing at me Nikhil grinned, sensing my state of dazed immobility.

"Do I need to tell you that?" I asked morosely.

"I thought it would be a nice break," he said, cupping my face in his hands.

"Please, not here! We should do this in private," I whispered urgently, sliding further into my chair.

He sat back. "I wanted to ask you something. I don't know if this is the right time and place but I would like to take our relation forward," he said cautiously,

The spectacle of struggle and achievement on the ground formed a fitting background for our conversation, which seemed destined to get intense and intimate. I eyed him speculatively.

He leaned closer and said, "I want to marry you."

I nodded eagerly, flushing, unable to believe what he had just said. My heart pounded with excitement to a seductive beat. Those five words sounded like music to me – deliberate, measured and erotic. It was the music of my whole life.

"We could adopt a baby girl," he suggested, his gaze bold and intent, assessing my response.

Ah! I wish everything had paused there, with us looking into each other's eyes and a bright spectacle serving as background.

"Why a girl?" My low voice shook with excitement.

He gave me a challenging, sensuous look. "Basically because I would like it, and secondly, to set the gender ratio right in our family," he jested.

"But no one will accept our marriage." It had become a habit of mine to go against what the moment offered.

"It is legal in Nepal. We could go there and spend our lives together. I just want to be with you, with no boundaries."

My inner goddess danced, stripped naked, ready to embrace this wonderful new reality. Love filled my being, deep and overwhelming.

"Are you really serious about this?" I still had my doubts.

"Do you doubt me?" he asked, taken aback. "I would not have returned had this not been on my mind."

"I do not doubt you, Niks. I am merely asking if you are prepared to take this step. You know your mother will not accept me or our relationship. I have nothing to lose; I have loose ties with my parents. Nor do they expect anything from me. It is a relationship which exits for our relations. I know I am sometimes weak, but nevertheless I am a maverick. I do not play by the rules others have made for me. But it matters for you, Nikhil. In this matter you have more at stake. What I lose is repairable; you have to weigh what it will cost you."

My words formed a long chain in his mind. He stared at me, a bittersweet smile on his lips.

"Will you marry me?" he asked softly, his gaze intent.

"Yes, I will," I answered, smiling away my inhibitions.

"From now on you need not worry," he stated definitely, putting his hand on mine.

"I have faith in you," I replied.

"Everything from now on will set our fate."

His words resonated in my ears. His decision had set our fate surely, but I had my share of reservations which I did not share with him. I knew my worst fears were like impending doom waiting to come true.

"Anu, I need you in my life," he said quietly. "I have lived loneliness while I was in Sierra Leone. Every day seemed a thorn in my side, making my eyes heavy and mind dreary. Just think, in six months and we shall be living together!"

I smiled, feeling intoxicated, my mind brimming with seamless thoughts, warmed by his love. "I could not have wished for anything more beautiful than this. I realise how I have grown in this journey with you and how much I want to remain in the circle of your love."

Dusk fell as the team that had never won a match managed to clinch its first victory — a sober 1-0 win from a penalty kick. The handful of supporters of the winning team roared loudly and perhaps by their definition, insanely. They had tasted victory, just like us.

***

I knew I was labelled 'different' and that it would define every moment of my life. I was unable to blend in with the others. I hated living a lie every day, laughing at gay jokes, all the time knowing the laugh was on me. I found it hard watching movies with implicit jokes about the community and seeing my sister's eyes turn towards me when the news showed something on LGBT rights. Often, when I stepped into my room I felt my skin burning to the touch. I sensed some people shrink away and the sympathy of others, but very few acted normal. My senses and desires were hidden behind curtains. All my actions and reactions were captured and catapulted by my gay identity. Nothing else mattered. Every day I sensed social ostracism. I struggled to recreate myself. My face was like a mask I wore to hide the real me. Endlessly I wondered if I was flawed by nature. Perhaps Dhriti was right, many people live with this truth without letting it out; they just live without questioning or being questioned. But I wanted to live and wear my truth in the hope that someday people would accept it.

***

It was a dark evening outside. The mist-laden breeze blew amorously, carrying savoury desires. I loved the anonymity the darkness gave me. The murky January clouds seemed to reflect my own foreboding for my mother had learnt of my sexual bias and relationship from my sister. She looked at me, the dreaded question in her eyes.

"I have heard something." There was disdain in her voice.

"You have heard it right." I wished to be as brief as possible, my voice a strange blend of curtness and reverence.

"I know whatever I say will not stop you from doing what you want to," she said, knowing my stubborn maverick nature.

"You know me well, mom." My rebellious tone made my intentions clear.

Her eyes met mine; there was both curiosity and motherly affection in their deep brown depths. "I am not here to advocate my views, son. Some things do fall outside the natural order; that is not wrong. It's just how the course of life is destined, packed with things desired and undesired, dreams and reality, acceptance and rejection. I am not angry with you, but as a mother and one who has lived longer on this earth than you, I am concerned for you my son. I cannot be objective."

"What do you mean by being objective?"

"Son, in life there are certain truths that are not told and taken to the grave. Consider this relationship as such a truth. When people talk, they will not just talk about you but about everyone around you, everyone you are related to." She seated herself beside me and placed a gentle hand on my shoulder. "Your choices affect us all, most importantly your sister. You may call me conservative, shallow minded or even unmindful of your feelings, but I consider myself a protective Indian mother who follows the brahmanical way of living. I am conservative and socially conscious. I am not against you; I respect your love and I appreciate that you have come forward to talk to us about this." She gave me a half smile before saying, "But I am equally concerned and fear the consequences."

I had been nodding as she spoke but now I looked at her and asked, "Consequences?"

"If you ever decide to open up, keep in mind that it will have repercussions for both you and for us."

"You don't want me to open up my dark secret?" I asked, a sarcastic smile on my face.

"Don't call it a dark secret if it is a pure and true emotion," she replied quietly, hugging me. "It is good to listen to the heart, but it is also important to know the society you live in."

I realized I had been holding my breath, awed by her understanding, empathy and support. I nodded, my face serious. "Thank you mom."

"Maybe it's just how things are."

"And you will never force me to take up the 'normal' life?" I asked.

She sighed and moved away. I could see her gaze turn pensive. "Are you sure you want this for the rest of your life?" she asked, her voice low. I nodded. She looked at me, her face expressionless. "Perhaps this happened because you have never tried being with a girl."

Her statement struck me like an indictment. I wondered if she would next ask me to try it before I finally decided.

"It was just a thought," she said cautiously.

My face darkened "Are you suggesting I try a girl?" I asked, the stark incompatible truths quivering in the air between us.

"At this age hormones speak louder than the mind or heart. If your hormones have drawn you into a relationship with a guy, you can also, if you want, respond to a girl. Maybe you will even like the softness of a girl more."

I silently ridiculed the idea, the hollowness of her suggestion. "Mom, I have never felt anything for any girl," I sighed wearily.

"You can if you try. After all, a man can only marry a woman."

"Not every guy must marry," I replied, calm but stern.

My mother's face was expressionless as she said, "Don't get me wrong. I was just suggesting you give a thought to trying a girl. Maybe it will take your mind from that guy. Think it over. I have heard there are websites that can help. Try getting into a relationship. Or if you find that difficult, try hooking up for some time. You may be surprised."

I listened but did not respond. I smiled inwardly at the irony of the situation. My mother would never have suggested such a thing had I been straight!

"Just think over it and try to mix with girls," she reiterated, suggesting I do the very thing that in the normal course would have been considered taboo in the family.

"If you say so I will try. But if nothing works out, what then?' I asked, the trace of a smile on my face.

"Then live your life the way you want to. I shall not object. I am just worried about the spillover and the impact it will have on all of us," she said softly. Giving me an affectionate half smile she walked towards the kitchen.

I was content my family understood me.

*****

14

With Him At Last

"Wake up! Gotta go in early today," Nikhil said, kissing me just below my ear.

I opened my eyes and turned to face him. He looked fresh and delicious as he leaned over me. "What time is it?" Still half asleep, I rubbed my eyes. I didn't want to be late either.

"No panic, it's not that late. I have a breakfast meeting so I must rush." He rubbed his nose against mine and gave me a quick peck.

"You smell good," I murmured, stretching out to him. My limbs felt pleasurably tight. Seeing that my attempt to get his attention went unnoticed, I pleaded, "Don't go!"

He cocked his head to one side and raised an eyebrow "Are you trying to seduce an honest, hardworking man and keeping him away from work? You are still in probation my dear, but my job gives us a living," he teased as he applied cream on his face for a shave.

I nodded sleepily, fixing my gaze on his bare body. He looked at me in the mirror and smiled. "I am tempted by both you and work but this morning I shall reserve the temptation to my work," he said. "What time will you be back from work?"

"Before that I need to make up my mind to attend office today. As you mentioned, I am still on probation," I murmured in a sleepy tone. "Why not bathe together and save water" I suggested innocently.

At any other time I could have expected an ardent response, but this morning was not that time.

"Nooo…" he brushed the idea aside. "While I bathe you can prepare breakfast. An omelette will work."

I prepared breakfast as he got ready. He hurried into the kitchen in a navy blue shirt and denims – the perfect casual but smart look.

"We can go out this evening, just to break the monotony," he suggested.

I nodded and said with a straight face. 'Maybe you can also suggest where to go."

"I'll come to your office and we can go from there. Completely your choice, no interference from me… Does that work?" he asked, immune to my tricks.

"Oh don't try getting cute with me. I know you will have your rulings and present your stupid ideas about a date in such a passionate manner that I will yield to them. Niks I love loving you but I hate going out with you."

His jaw dropped open. I wished he would say, 'Your wish is my command, Anu'. A thrill ran through me. He has a way of diverting such conversation into the most romantic endings.

He stepped towards me, smiled and took the breakfast plate from my hands. Shaking his head he said, "Then I will see you doing what you do the best with me."

He wore such a seductive smile that my stomach tightened at once. He took another step, grasped me in one easy swoop and swatted my behind. I clung to him in pleasure as he kissed me passionately. My hands moved involuntarily to undo the first button of his shirt. He groaned against my mouth and then pulled away reluctantly.

"Let me go now!" he said, hastily buttoning his shirt.

"Then have your breakfast." I turned away, hiding a smile.

He had a decent job in hand at an advertising firm, while I was still struggling to ground myself. Anyway I was enjoying myself living lavishly on his enviable salary. After college I had moved in with him into his rented studio apartment, defying every ordeal my parents faced in the little society they lived in. I had learned and unlearned many lessons since Niks had stepped into my world. His scorching looks, silken hugs and boyish tantrums had turned me into a rebel. Love is cruel; it turns you into a different being.

I knew I would have to move out once his mother arrived from his hometown. He had not opened up to her despite her misgivings about him. I was the only fool to have done that. But it gave me the liberty I had always yearned for. More than anything else, I missed my sister. We had talked on numerous occasions after that first episode. We did try to respect each other's views, but it was difficult to take flight together so we went in opposite directions. My mother had the notion that marrying me off would cure me and make me like other guys in the family. My father considered me to be diseased and despised me. Things had shifted from neutral to reverse gear in my life. I wished I could burst the bubble my family was living in; the flimsy shell created of their beliefs.

I never pushed Nikhil about opening up to his mother about our relationship; I feared the consequences. But I feared the consequences of not opening up as well. His mother also lived in a bubble, much like my family did. I had chosen my destiny and often told myself there was nothing left to lose…bubbles had to burst some time.

After performing my daily ritual of cleaning the house, putting the dirty laundry to one side in the hope that I would get it done one fine day, watering the newly planted lilies in the small balcony we proudly possessed, and offering last evening's leftovers to the three-legged dog Manjula, who roamed our neighborhood, I set off for my lively office, a FM radio station, with a free mind. I was late, again, but I could smell freedom in the air — freedom from my past, from questions, rituals, beliefs and obligations. I had taken a step forward, never to turn back.

I worked at the FM station as a script-writer and also dedicated some of my time to my own writing. This was a place where no one knew me; they always greeted me with smiles. I must have been the youngest there and perhaps the cutest; some called me a natural charmer. They knew how to play with words, it was their job. My job was to add spice.

Nikhil never failed to call me in the afternoon to enquire how I was doing. Have you had your food…how's the day going… He loved me as a lover and guarded me as a guardian. Actually, he didn't care for where I worked and often asked if I intended to change my job after probation ended. But I was adamant about playing by my own rules. And the job fuelled my creative yen. Being on probation I wore multiple hats — assistant, executive, note-taker, business analyst, and if they permitted, script writer. But in less I had gained more. I had stepped out and met new people, no longer carrying the baggage of my past. I was learning new things and unlearning some past teachings. And secretly I searched for someone like me, perhaps to form a little group of our own. Nikhil knew many in the gay community, but he was the only one I knew. I wanted to expand my small world but I had neither the traits nor the clues to make me successful in this.

***

That evening Nikhil hugged me as he came in; I guessed his meeting had been successful.

"So how was it?" I asked.

"Couldn't have gone better," was the instant reply. "How was your day?"

"Oh, I spent half the day taking notes, then editing some stuff and doing whatever else I'm supposed to be doing there." My words seemed to come like a volley from a loose cannon as I clenched my teeth and shook my head, my exasperation palpable.

He gazed at me intently. "You have the most incorruptible mind I know," he said, closing his eyes and shaking his head in disbelief.

I couldn't resist giving him a smile, all my irritation gone in a second.

"It's just another month to completing probation, then you can think of joining somewhere else."

"But I love the real work, when I get to do it," I said, my voice assertive and earnest. It was engaging and frustrating at the same time.

"Then so be with it," he said, throwing an arm over my shoulder. "I'm happy as long as you are." He took one of my hands and placed it over his heart. "Here's the place for you."

His heart was beating frantically and mine began to pound in a deperate desire to match the beat. His eyes remained fixed on me, his jaw tense. "So are you game?" he whispered in my ear.

"Game for what?" I teased. The sight of him offering himself to me was a clarion call to my inner goddess.

He ran his fingers through my hair, grasped my head and tilted it back. Looking into my eyes he asked again, "Are you game?"

"Yes…" I breathed.

***

"Tell me our whole life is going to be this way," I said, my voice throbbing with intensity.

"Why, you have some doubt?" he asked, glancing at me.

"I just want to be sure."

"It will be — for sure."

Nikhil cupped my face and gazed at me intently for a moment. I reached up, my fingers pressed against his.

"I have left everyone to be with you," I said in a choked voice, feeling a sudden rush of tears. For days, months indeed, I had not felt like this. Why now?

He pulled himself, clasped my hand and gently said, "You are my lifeline. I will always be with you,"

We were locked in an inseparable embrace. I felt his warm, skin beneath my lips, its sweet smell filling my senses. Our eyes met, offering consolation and comfort. I realized then that though we had grown in our relationship, yet a figment of fear continued to haunt me. Somehow I always felt I would lose him. I moaned in ecstacy and inner trepidation as he lifted my face so that our lips met and held as if we would never let go in this world or the next.

But I feared things would slip; afraid of the looming future. Somewhere, sometime, something…I didn't know what but I feared it. He saw it in my eyes but compelled me to live in the present. But I nursed the fear of losing him.

*****

15

Some Past Chapters Again

It did not take me time to gather the scattered pieces of my professional life. From a part-time note-taker, secretary and script writer, I graduated with ease to a full-time script writer and part-time RJ. Everything came to me in a flash. It started when my boss asked me to host an early morning show. Started as an experiment, we tasted success with every move we made. And gradually things flowed, took shape and got organized. I never auctioned Nikhil's suggestion to try something else. I stayed with my FM job and it clicked. It took me some time to establish myself but when it happened I enjoyed, honoured and nursed that space.

Nikhil too, had with earnest efforts established himself in his firm. I sometimes wondered if he remembered that Sierra Leone stint covering war crimes; or had it just been a wasted journey for him? He had gone from war reporting to advertising. His face sometimes said, 'It hardly matters'. I sometimes laughed and sometimes pondered life's ironies.

As usual I reached home before him that day. My mind blank, I called my sister, after months. I didn't remember when I had last spoken to her. Following her marriage we had developed an estranged animosity. Due to my father's unhealed anger, my relations with everyone in the family turned cold. At the start I often spoke with my sister and sometimes my mother took the phone from her and spoke too. I missed them and they missed me, but we had learnt to live without each other. I was happy with Nikhil and they without me. My sister got married and my presence was unnoticed in the family. But a part of me still lived in Didi's shadow, holding onto memories, not wanting time to slip by.

"Hi bro, how are things?" she said in a barely audible voice, the background noise loud and clear. She had left her job to practice spiritual healing.

"I'm good. I heard things are not good in your marriage," I said tentatively.

"My life's in a bin. Cool that you chose what you wanted. Hard decisions turn sweeter with time," she told me, a familiar strain in her voice. "I'm seeking a divorce. I'm just not made for marriage."

"Sorry it turned out so bad."

"No need to be sorry buddy, I just weigh my chances with this guy right. He is a good man but I just couldn't get into it. Now I desperately want to come out of it; can't hold on any longer. The longer I stay the more I will destroy his life." She paused, recalling forlorn moments. There was a note of guilt in her voice, something foreign to her. "But I'm glad you are happy. I was always concerned about you, though I couldn't express it." Her tone changed with the topic of conversation.

"Don't think that I didn't feel your concern. By the way, I called to ask if we could meet?"

'Sure, any day you say…tomorrow? If it works for you we could meet at our same old place."

"Fine, tomorrow works. It's been days and days. I've moved on in life but I always want to turn back to steal some moments from the past that I spent with you."

"I'll be happy to meet you too. I'm sort of pissed off with my life and want to relive my past."

"And I have a future to look towards."

"I'd be glad to know your future plans."

"Nothing concrete right now."

"Hey, I'll catch up with you tomorrow. I've some knowledge seekers waiting outside."

"Sure Di…bye." I put down the phone.

It would be hours before Nikhil returned. I switched on the air-conditioner and got down to reading – Japanese culture this time. I had developed quite an affinity towards Buddhist teachings and Japan, being a Buddist epicenter, fascinated me. Japanese traditions can be bewildering at times. They have an innovative way of pleasing their guests; a woman shares a bath with the guest to please him and soon the whole family joins in. Sounds erotic. I find nakedness sublime if one can really appreciate it. There is no hypocrisy; it is like romancing nature and the self, coming to terms with the real you. Cultures are so strange in that what is revered in one place is seen as unholy in another. Nevertheless, culture defines us. Hindu mythology is full of incidents of homosexuality, as are the scriptures; it is carved on temple walls. Yet we continue to fear and abhor it, choosing to turn a blind eye to its existence in society and scripture.

I shut the book and closed my tired eyes. The awkward silence of the summer evening was replaced by a cacophony of vehicles heading home after the working day. Nikhil would be in one such car with his colleagues, who had formed a carpool. He would get down at the outer ring turn and take an auto home. I made some coffee. Taking out my diary I began to scribble my thoughts. Closing my mind to outer distractions I set off to chase my thoughts from their hiding places. The apartment was plunged in deep silence, a delicious break from the hustle-bustle of my work place. This was time for me – my thoughts, my writing. Soon Nikhil would be back and I would then have to wait till he fell asleep to be with myself again. I wrote on…

It was 7:30pm, time for Nikhil to return. I showered quickly and put on a t-shirt he had bought me. He always grumbled about my poor dress sense. I put it on, the fabric skimming my skin and clinging to my body. It was fine cotton, perfect for this weather, and a delight for the eyes. I felt luxurious and elegant. I waited for him to return.

Another fifteen minutes and the doorbell rang. I opened the door to find him smiling his usual 'I missed you all day' grin. He didn't notice the t-shirt. I handed him a towel saying, "Have a shower, you must be tired. I'll get something to eat."

He smiled, his eyes following me. His hands reached for me as he said, "Do you have any idea how good you look in that t-shirt?"

So he had noticed it after all. "This was a gift from you," I reminded him.

He took off his shirt and held out his arms, ready to enfold me. "Go and shower!" I shrieked, merely to break the spell.

"Give me a shower," he suggested, taking a step forward and putting his arms around my waist.

'Nooo… you freshen up; I'll prepare something to eat."

Deaf to my words he wrapped himself around me and nuzzled my neck.

"How do you manage to be so romantic, after the whole day, and the Delhi traffic?" I murmured breathlessly, throwing my head back in pleasure.

"I have no idea; you make me forget everything," he retorted, throwing up his hands.

I was left smiling like a kid with a butterfly in his hand. "Now go and shower…you smell of sweat," I pushed him off, crashing his thoughts of a little romance. "I'm making a burger for you. Now go and shower."

He turned away with a smile, heading for the bathroom. Inspecting the impressive contents of the fridge, I decided to go for a healthy bean salad and banana shake. It would be quick and easy and tastier than a burger. Nikhil loved a long lazy shower on hot summer days. It would give me ample time to experiment.

My mind was abuzz with ideas. I had never set limits when it came to pleasing him. So I turned on his favourite music, sashayed back to the kitchen and found a bowl, peeled the bananas, got milk from the fridge, turned on the juicer and began to whisk, dancing to the loud beat of the music. Raiding the fridge once more, I gathered two boiled potatoes, sprouts, onions, cucumber and tomatoes. A perfect recipe was in the making. Finding a pan, I placed it on the stove and put in a little safflower oil and fried some finely chopped onions till they turned golden. Then I put in the other ingredients – a healthy snack for a tired soul.

Once the bean salad was almost ready to be served, I got some finely chopped coriander leaves and a lemon for the final seasoning. My love for Niks and food had made me into a fine chef. I switched off the extra lights in the apartment to set the right mood.

Nikhil appeared wrapped in a towel, water droplets still clinging to his body like drops of nectar. I felt a rush of desire, reveling in the thought that he was mine. It brought a delighted smile to my face.

"I changed my plans and opted for a healthy diet," I announced.

A soft smile played on his lips. "Aha…it looks good. Assorted beans have always been a favourite of mine," he said, sitting down on the fine sofa we had bought just a week ago. I felt strangely winded. It was hard taking my eyes off him; it always had been. I held him by the forearms and planted a soft kiss on his wet shoulder.

"You look so elegant in that t-shirt that I really don't feel like taking it off you," he breathed.

His words, as usual, brought a smile to my face and set my heart racing. "Does that mean we don't have plans today?" My mouth quirked down at my foolish reply.

He smiled too, dexterously planted a soft kiss on my parted lips. I was captivated by the potent combination of his masculine beauty and raw sexuality. "I have a different plan for you today," he laughed.

My desires were like leaping flames but I controlled myself, disengaging myself and picking up a spoon to have my share of the salad.

"This is good," he said appreciatively.

"That's because I made it," I stated proudly, sitting cross-legged and consuming the fresh salad.

His mouth twisted into a smile. "Did your mother teach you to cook?" he asked.

"Not really. Rather it was my own instincts and desire to please you. I want to take care of you."

'Me too,' he replied, undefinable emotion in his voice.

My heart raced. '*Achcha*, before I forget, I had to tell you something," I said. Once I had his whole attention, I announced, "Aarya and Dhriti are getting married in December."

"Oh, that's good news! So you get to party on both sides?"

"*We* get to party." My brow furrowed as I emphasized *we*.

"Are they living together?" he asked.

"Sort of…yes. Aarya has a rented room and Dhriti lives in a hostel but visits and often stays back. They are still not earning great but I believe they will be able to manage together. You are the only one who earns big," I teased.

"That's because they are in the media business and I am on the creative side of advertising," he replied calmly.

'Whatever…your earnings give me the option of flushing away large sums of money in shopping."

"It's all yours," he said, bowing his naked torso.

I looked at him. If only the heart could speak… "Now allow me to plan dinner. I can feel your wrong intentions," I said, taking a dig at him.

"Wrong!" he exclaimed. "Hey, they are the most right of intentions – loving the beautiful thing you have with you. Looking at you all day long would be a luxury for me."

With that he pulled me into an embrace and gave me a quick peck on my lips. Pulling the towel wrapped around his waist, he dropped it onto the floor. "I need you," he whispered in my ear.

"You're getting feisty ol' man."

"Yes, I am. You turn me on." He softly nuzzled my earlobe.

He looked so freaking hot, lively and carefree. His eyes seemed to say 'dinner can wait, not I'. He walked over to the fridge and brought back a pint of ice-cream. Climbing smoothly back onto the sofa, he first peeled off my T-shirt and then the lid of the ice cream carton. I could guess what came next. He scooped out a spoonful and offered it to me. I opened my mouth and took in the freezing dollop, knowing it was just the start of the game.

"Do you like it?" he asked casually.

"Oh yes!" I said, easing myself back on the sofa.

He scooped out another spoonful and asked me to feed him. I followed him, as usual. He took another spoonful from the tub and then reached out to touch my lips. He let the ice cream slowly melt on the spoon and dripped onto my throat and then onto my chest. He bent and lasciviously licked it off, leaving me longing for more. My body felt hot and cold at the same time. The game of odds had begun.

"It tastes even better this way," Nikhil said softly as he took another spoon, let it melt and drip onto his chest. I dipped down and licked the sweetness off his body. He moaned with desire. It did taste better that way. He took another spoonful and dribbled it onto my nipples. He spread the ice cream with the back of the spoon, and then deliberately sucked it off me, playfully biting my nipples. His mouth was hot, the ice cream cool. We kept repeating turns and soon a white rivulet ran onto the sofa. We kissed, his skilled, now ice cold tongue rolling over mine, tasting heavenly.

Pushing me down so that I lay on the sofa, he trailed a spoonful of ice-cream onto my navel. A soft, chilly, irresistible sensation hit me. He ran his tongue across my belly and sucked my navel. Aphrodite took possession of me as he sucked my nipples first and then followed the trail of ice-cream, sucking hard and biting gently as he went. It was impossible to resist the glory of my goddess. It was her day. I gyrated to the rhythm as he suckled my navel. It was exhilarating caught in a sweet, chilly spell as his tongue whisked over my navel. I was panting, wet with desire.

"Do you like it?" he breathed, his tongue worked its magic.

I had always hated obvious questions. But I revelled in the fact that I could give him so much pleasure. He was inside me, the melted ice-cream spread over my body. An odd sensation hit me as he got harder and quicker. It hurt but I didn't complain; the pain was somehow soothing. I wanted him with every fibre of my being. He continued till he was left breathless. I kissed him on the forehead as he finally rested his head on my chest.

***

The intense session was to be followed by an intimate dinner. I cooked mushroom, sautéed with onion and ginger, peanuts and coriander.

Nikhil stepped into the kitchen, a sad look on his face. "Come on baby, I'm hungry," he complained.

"It's done," I replied happily, silly-happy.

He wound his arms around me from behind and pressed against my back.

"Nikhil, put on a movie while I get dinner."

"Sure…as you command."

When I took in the food, I saw he had chosen *Four Christmases,* a romantic comedy.

"I'm happy for Aarya and Dhriti," I said to him. "I still remember my long whiskey sessions with Aarya, when he would narrate his story to me. It was a case of love at first sight for him. I could never imagine him being serious about anyone but he kept proving me wrong."

"Well, Dhriti is a good girl to get serious about. She is smart, understanding, pretty – everything a guy looks for in a girl," Nikhil commented.

"You know Dhriti had a crush on you," I told him.

"And I always thought it was you she liked. She was always close to you."

"I had a big time crush on Aarya," I chuckled, feeling as proud as a child with his favourite toy.

"Really? When was that?"

"Before and even while I was with you. I couldn't resist ogling at his perfect body. Didn't *you* find him attractive?"

"He is, for that matter. Why didn't you try with him?"

"He didn't have that instinct. And then, when you came into my life, after I had spent so many days stalking you, I was the happiest person with everything I could ask for."

"But didn't you say you wanted him then too?"

"Obviously…if you had such a perfectly shaped guy in your room in boxers, wouldn't it turn you on as well?"

"So if he were to come to you today and ask you to spend a night with him, you could easily be turned on?" he growled suspiciously.

The discussion was going nowhere."Nikhil you are getting me wrong, completely wrong. Don't mess with the facts," I said.

"I was just thinking about our future," he retorted.

"Have I ever brought your past into our present? I only liked him, you have slept with other people, but have I ever brought that into our lives?" I argued, my tone wounded and accusatory.

"That was over way before you came into my life. If I had wanted I could have slept with someone else." His voice rose along with his temper.

"Did I sleep with him? I just liked him, that's all. Let's please end this conversation," I pleaded.

He looked at my moist eyes. We had argued probably for the first time since we had been living together. He bent forward wiped the tears off my cheeks. Hugging me he asked me to forgive him. And I asked him to forgive and forget as well; all arguments and anger melted into smiles and kisses.

"Let's have dinner now." he whispered.

"Don't do it ever again," I muttered, feeling like a child from whom his favourite toy had been taken.

"I'm sorry I argued. You do so much for me."

"Now eat, it's your favourite dish," I replied, serving him generously from the dish.

The whole argument evaporated as he ate hungrily. The anguish melted and the atmosphere in the room became one of sweet reunion.

"You are a dominating ass," I muttered.

He gave me a dazzling, full toothed, happy-go-lucky smile. I couldn't help it, seeing his sheer joy I smiled too. He leaned forward and *shit!*, pulled my cheeks. I rolled my eyes, wanting to remind him angrily that I was a 24-year-old, not a nursery kid. Before I could do so, he rubbed his nose against mine and whispered, "As ever, you are unexpected". His eyes danced with humour. I bit my lip, a soft smile spreading across my face as I gazed back at him.

***

Nikhil was on the phone; he looked troubled. *Could be an office issue*, I thought and shifted my focus back to the movie. After fifteen minutes he came back, threw his mobile onto the bed and sat down next to me.

"So what happened in the movie?" he asked.

"Good dialogues but poor story line. Just listen and enjoy it, don't overload your brain," I said in a sleepy voice, stretching my legs.

"Rom-coms are meant for that — a feast of good one-liners and worry not where the story and characters take you," he agreed.

"Thankfully it's not boring" I said, leaning against him.

For minutes we didn't say anything more and focused on the movie. Nikhil had his hand rested on my chest as I lay across him.

"There's a problem," he finally said, sounding grave. From his tone I guessed it was about us.

"Problem as in some official thing?" I asked casually.

"My mother wants to come and live with me for some time." He shook his head, his expression serious.

"Any idea for how long? I can move in with my sister for the duration".

"No idea. I'm worried about something else – she talked of marriage. What should I say? How can I open up to her?"

I looked at him. All levity had disappeared from his face, his eyes dark and intense; he was seriously worried. So my fears had come true. I had not wanted him to open up and have to cut all relations with his family like I had, but if he did not speak up our relationship would get buried. Something had to give. He cupped my face in his hands, as if desperately trying to find an answer there. I kissed him softly. I knew this had to come and it had... those amorphous fears...

"Take my word, don't open up. I was never on great terms with my parents so it was easier for me. Your case is different; don't repeat that mistake," I said in a low voice.

"Then what should I do? Ruin lives – mine, yours and that of some girl? I can't do that!" He closed his eyes, distressed and distraught.

I exhaled. "So you're thinking of opening up?"

"I don't know. It's not happening right away but someday soon the question will come up."

He was right. Someday the question would arise and answers would have to be given. People would demand explanations.

"Your mother would like to stay with you. You'll have to shift to a more spacious place."

"Anu, that's not the issue! What about us?"

"I can rent a place. The way we are here, we can be there. See Nikhil, we knew this was bound to happen sooner or later so there's no point crying over it. Nothing is going to change our beautiful relationship."

"But that doesn't solve my problem." He was clearly frustrated.

Though riddled with doubt within, my lips turned up in a quirky smile to reassure and relax him. "Well, that's the great thing about being a faint-heart. You like to pre-plan things. I have woken and slept with these questions and the only plausible answer seems to be to let it happen and live a dual life. We will still have each other and our life."

"How Anu?"

"You'll have a conditional marriage, which will end in divorce," I muttered, gazing into his dark, serious eyes.

He was not convinced. "That is easy to plan but hard to implement. It depends on the other person's will. Also, the price paid can be very heavy. It's not a practical plan," he stated, the corporate guy in him sounding stern.

"Marry a lesbian." I stood up as I made the stark suggestion, my eyes wide and deathly pale.

He looked at me, smiled nervously at what my usually timid mind had concocted.

"Are you serious?"

"This is not a time for jokes." *I was serious*. "To me it seems a safe option – safe for the girl too. Neither she nor you will expect anything from each other. Who is to know what does not happen in the bedroom?" I said, shrugging my shoulders.

"Do you really think it's wise?"

"It's sane. You not only save us, you save her and her partner as well. She would be faced with an almost impossible dilemma – far worse than our own. You can support each other, and most importantly our relationship remains, her relationship remains, and we all get to live our lives. If your mother never knows the truth, which is entirely possible, she remains happy too. And what happens in the bedroom remains in the bedroom."

"I have to say the plan isn't stupid."

"I'm happy you think so. Will your mother stay with you always?" I asked, mulling things over in my mind.

"It's a remote possibility."

"In that case, make frequent 'travel' plans and come and stay with me. I hope that sounds like quite a deal."

"It still doesn't sound a full-fledged plan." He looked eager yet worried at the same time.

Lost in deep thought, he stood looking out of the window at the never-ending Delhi traffic. What I had suggested required great audacity, but I was ready to take any daring step to keep rather than lose him. I poured him a glass of cold water. He looked at me, his eyes harbouring some deep, unknown fear. For the first time it was I who emanated confidence. Putting a hand on his shoulder I smiled. I could see the confusion in him but he held out his arms and enfolded me, warmth, relief and regret spreading from one to the other.

'It's not that hard' I whispered, glancing up at the moon in the sky. "We have limited options. Either you marry a girl and cheat by having a relationship with me, or open up to your mother and remain with me."

"The first I will not do and the second I can not do."

"Life is never going to be easy for us. Think about what I've said; it's manageable and will keep everyone happy."

"I feel so confused."

"Don't be. It's just a thought; keep it with you. When the time comes, take your decision." A bittersweet smile tugged at my lips.

There was something in both of us that mirrored each other. He nodded his head and gave me a quick smile. We could both hear the winds of change blowing behind us.

***

When I opened my eyes, light had filled the room, making me blink. My head was fuzzy, probably from lack of sleep. I had a late work shift but I had made plans to meet my sister. I reluctantly put aside the enticement of more sleep and got up.

"Good morning!" Nikhil was fully dressed, all set to leave. "I thought you'd sleep late, so I didn't wake you. Anyway, I've made some breakfast for you," he said, smiling affectionately.

"Thanks," I murmured, glad I was up to see him off.

I wandered into the kitchen to have a look at the breakfast he had made. I was lavish. Feeling overwhelmed by the love poured on me, I scuttled towards the bathroom and hurriedly got ready to go and meet my sister after such a long time. As I took sips of coffee, recollections of the days we had spent together flashed through my mind. To me she had always been more than my mother. And then, in last two years, relations between us had turned from warm to frigid. I had made this move in the hope that we could thaw the ice and turn back the clock to a time when we meant so much to each other.

On the metro I flipped through the newspaper. There had been a Gay Pride in Australia. Society there was more liberal, I consoled myself. In India, things are somewhat better in Mumbai, but in Delhi, queer culture is still hidden, unappreciated, unrecognized and not talked about in conservative family circles. Most people laugh it off unknown to the idea that their own family might have a gay or lesbian member. It was safer to ignore the truth or, like my mother, suggest that sleeping with the opposite sex would miraculously rid one of the burden of being gay. I wanted to say it was biological; that some people are born that way. I looked at the photograph in the paper again, hoping desperately that India would one day be a liberal, developed society.

I got down at Hauz Khas. Didi was waiting for me. I hopped into her car and we wove our way through the busy streets to our old rendezvous – a humble coffee bar, where we had often sat to have coffee and do our assignments away from the loud parental arguments at home. We had lived a part of our lives here. In fact, I had once brought Aarya and Dhiriti here to introduce them to Didi. *Old memories lived on.*

"You are allowed to say something," Didi said.

My face fell and my lips pressed into a thin line. "You can begin the conversation too, you know."

"Very well; how are you then?"

"I'm good. How are you?" I was still smarting.

"That's good to hear. I hope Nikhil is taking care of you," she said, taking a speedy left turn.

"He is. So have you made up your mind to go ahead with a divorce?" I enquired.

"I've put in the papers; it's becoming impossible to stay together. One simply cannot keep going through the same sullen cycle of events every day. It's hard for him too. He's a nice guy after all."

"So what exactly happened?"

We had arrived in front of the coffee house so she said, "Go in. I'll park the car and join you."

Old times seemed to come alive as I walked in and took over a corner table. A few minutes later Didi came in and sat down opposite me. A waiter came up to pour water into two glasses from a jug and then left.

"They still don't have a menu card," I commented.

"This place hasn't changed in years. When was the last time you came?"

"Three years ago, if I remember correctly. It doesn't look like things have changed. The same old posters of Bob Marley and Lennon and a fine collection of Beatles songs," I said, glancing around.

"Anyway, let's order coffee and sandwiches."

"I'm always in the mood for sandwiches," I said, rolling up my sleeves.

She summoned a waiter and gave him our order. Then she looked at me. "Now tell, how are things?"

"Mostly fine. Nikhil's mother is coming to visit."

"Does that mean you'll have to move out?"

"Most probably, but that isn't the problem. I'm afraid she is going to initiate talks about his marriage," I revealed, furrowing my brow.

"I hope you two have something planned. Is he going to tell his mother about your relationship?"

"I'm not in favour of that," I snapped. "You of all people know how it goes with others. It took us a lot of time to be reconciled, and as for our parents, I haven't seen them since the day I left the house to live with Nikhil. I don't want that to happen to him." I was deadly serious.

"I understand your concern," she replied quietly. "I don't think you'll do anything stupid, but please do not take any risks." Her voice was rough with concern.

I nodded. The waiter brought us coffee and sandwiches.

"So have you thought of what to do?" she asked, taking a sip of her scalding coffee.

"We had a discussion yesterday. It's too early still but we have thought of a few things," I mumbled.

"And what are those things; tell me only if you wish to."

"Nothing concrete yet. It's perhaps better we let things fructify a little before disclosing them." I waited for her reaction, my brows ceased.

She took a deep breath, two sips of coffee, a full bite of her sandwich and then looked at me, her eyes piercing. "You have a habit of leaving me clueless," she said.

"We just discussed it yesterday. Nothing has been settled. But we will do what is good for both of us. I don't want him to open up and risk souring his family relationships. He's an only child and his mother is a widow."

"You two are the right people to decide what to do. But do something that saves you from many explanations. Well it seems to me that you are ready to live a dual life." No one could call my sister obtuse; she was as sharp as a needle.

"I've never said no to a dual life. Frankly I have accepted this duality as part of my life," I smiled, relieved to have shared the truth.

"I'm sorry I turned against you when you told me about your relationship and I told mom about it. I held the view then that whatever was outside the norm needed to be corrected. I nursed such wrong ideas, such stupid views. When you left, I realized I had lost a valuable thing in my life. I realized you had taken right decision for your life." She reached out and put a hand over mine.

Ah! I had always hated her sentimentality. "It's okay Di, you don't have to keep blaming yourself for something I have long forgotten. I have a good habit of not recording such awful episodes in my diary," I said, amusement in my voice.

"That explains why you've got this far. There's a fair amount of the decision-maker in you."

I was genuinely amused. "I deny that!" I said earnestly, shrugged my shoulders.

"That's your modesty," she commented amicably.

"So how is everything at home?" I asked.

She looked at me, took a deep breath and said, "It's a pacified battlefield now. Mom and Dad should separate rather than continue to ruin each other's life. Let's talk about something else, this subject is past praying for."

"Like our childhood? Tell me what's wrong in *your* life?"

"Nothing!" she cried, shaking her head vehemently. "I think it's all going in the right direction now. I'm all set to live life on my own terms; no more compromises in the name of love, marriage or family." There was an ironic look in her eyes.

I smiled at her. *She too, had the habit of leaving me clueless.* "I suppose that's fair. No need to keep standing where you know you will be hurt or could hurt others."

"You understand…"

We ordered another round of coffee and talked about the old days. There's a certain poetry in memories. We enjoyed the moments as we sat in comfortable, companionable silence in that coffee bar – the place that had seen us grow up and mature.

***

That evening Nikhil was his usual self. He had some nagging issues to address – his mother wished to see him married and he had been asked to shift to Mumbai for work. The first was a tough one but the second he was trying to 'manage'. He had informed his seniors that he was reluctant to move away from Delhi. Despite all this, he brought home a loving smile.

"You're tense this evening. Tell me what the matter is," I said, looking at his drooping head as he sat on the sofa.

He immediately looked up. "Nothing really! There are loads of things to worry about anyway. Are you sure about what you suggested?" he asked a little doubtfully.

"I am. But you seem doubtful."

"Actually I haven't given it a serious thought" he replied vaguely.

"Really?" I knew he was lying.

He nodded. "I'm still not certain about the idea."

"And you think I am?" I asked, lifting an eyebrow. "I am not, but there seems no other way out."

"If I were to agree to your idea, how would we find the lesbian someone to play the other part in this?"

I sensed rather than heard a certain panic in what he said. "Well, how did you find the guy you had a relationship with before me?" I asked and waited for his reply.

"You mean social networking sites?"

"There are other options like getting connected with organizations that work on such issues or an LGBT club." I could see I had caught his attention.

"And what have you decided for yourself?"

Now that was a real bouncer. The fact was I had not decided anything for myself. "Well nothing yet," I temporized. "And if this arrangement goes well, I may not have to. Let's give it a try. It's the best we can do to save our relationship." I had never been more serious about anything in my life.

He looked at me for a long moment and then nodded, a smile lifting the corners of his mouth.

*****

16
ANOTHER DATE, ANOTHER TIME

After a filling meal at Utopia, Nikhil drove us back to my apartment, with ABBA's mesmerizing music coming over the speakers. It made for a peaceful interlude. In all it had been a mind-blowing day. We had been on a double date with Rati and her girlfriend Niharika joining us for dinner.

The months had seen quick changes in our lives, both big and small. There was now a certain momentum and direction to events, impossible to halt. Destiny seemed to have taken over our lives. When I had presented my quirky idea, Nikhil gave it due thought and we agreed it was the way forward. His mother moved in shortly thereafter and I moved out to a small, sublet. Talk of Nikhil's marriage took centre stage growing gradually more intense. I remember the day Nikhil told me about it. We were in my little flat, sitting on the sofa with his arm over my shoulders. I reiterated the plan. Seeing no other option open to him, he agreed we should go ahead.

There followed the crucial search for a girl who would be eager to be part of this plan. Neither of us personally knew a lesbian couple. I decided to discuss the issue with Aarya; he seemed the only possible person who could help us.

"Are you serious?" he asked, astonished by the whole story.

"It seems like a survival plan," I replied.

"Not foolproof however."

"I know. Can you think of something else?" I asked, utterly serious.

"I hope you people have thought this over carefully."

"Sure Aarya, we have. Nikhil was unsure at first but then bought the idea. For me, it's the result of a lot of deliberation."

"Then let's go to a LGBT club or get connected to someone through an NGO. I believe you've done the research?"

I nodded. "Both are possible but I would prefer the former, it would give me more opportunity to know people."

"I have never doubted your decisions Anu. You are not one to let go of things halfway."

"Thanks for standing by us."

"So let me know when and where we need to go. I have no issues about coming along if you think my presence will add value," he offered, a hint of uncertainty in his voice.

"Hey, now don't talk like that. I need you there with me this Sunday, in Chanakyapuri, where The Pride is to meet."

"Okay buddy, I'll be there."

My face finally broke into a wide smile. There is little to compare in the world to a true friend. "Thanks," I said. "It's been so long since we last met, I miss your company. Plus, the liquor quotient in my body has reduced considerably. That's not a healthy sign for a guy my age."

The whiskey was the perfect accompaniment to our catch-up session. He was excited about his forthcoming marriage. The date had been decided and the shopping carnival was to begin soon. I sense danger here, knowing I would be dragged willy-nilly on shopping expeditions on both sides. It seemed inevitable; I knew them better than they knew each other. But I cared more about the coming Sunday, hoping to set my life on a smooth sailing course.

***

Our destination was an ambient club in Chanakyapuri, where the group met on the first Sunday of every month. It turned out to be by far the best thing that had happened to me; I met people who thought as I did. Nikhil was not interested and chose to spend the weekends at home or going on a food trail, a south Indian food trail that is. He did not want to face the group. Perhaps he was hiding something but I did not ask. The other guy in my life, Aarya, accompanied me sometimes. Frankly I had never expected him to do that but it gave me a lot of moral support and I began to trust him implicitly. He had always been a guy I secretly loved anyway.

The mood in the group was upbeat. Everyone had his/her story to tell while the others were happy to listen. There were stories of honey-traps, harassment, social boycott, those who had been ditched and dumped. There were also the stories of long vacations, first dates and child adoptions. I could sense that everyone there felt a certain vacuum in their lives.

The group had a decent membership; some came from the high end of society. People came for different reasons – to look for dating options, to share experiences, or simply to feel lighter. I realized that many carried the burden of guilt and remorse, not about their sexual identity but because of social unacceptance. Others seemed indifferent. I really don't know which category I fell into.

I met Rati there. A young, elegant and brainy lawyer, she must have been the cynosure for all eyes in court. She seemed like the perfect choice.

"Nikhil's mother would be proud of his son's 'choice'," I murmured in Aarya's ear.

He grinned, his eyes fixed on Rati. "Sure will be," he said.

I wasn't sure how to approach her with what I had in mind. After all I was just a stranger. Finally I invited her for coffee on the pretext of seeking legal advice. No one denies a client and we fixed a meeting at a quiet café.

The next day Rati and I arrived exactly on time but Nikhil hurried in somewhat laggardly.

"Hey! I'm sorry I'm late; I was in a client meeting." He pulled out a chair and sat down, throwing Rati a quick look.

"You aren't all that late, so don't worry," I piped in, keen to set an amicable tone to the talks.

"So what should we have?" he asked casually.

"We've already had a round of coffee, but I'm game for another. How about you, Rati?"

"Sure, legal talk is always best over coffee."

Nikhil looked up and smiled. The girl was quick.

"Well, it's not just legal, there's more to the talks," I said.

"Interesting…please begin."

"Rati, we are a couple," I said, pointing to Nikhil and me. Now I had her attention. "And we wanna be together. The issue is that Nikhil's mother wants him to be married, to a girl of course. This would destroy both his and the girl's life. If he opens to his mother instead, that would have equally disastrous consequences." I halted, wanting to hear what she had to say before going any further.

"We all go through such situations; I understand," she said in a low voice.

"What do *you* think could be a solution?"

"It's not a legal problem, Anuj. You don't need a legal help to sort this out."

The coffee arrived – freshly brewed cappuccino. Picking up my cup I said, "But we do need you as a person. Perhaps you face a similar situation? Please place yourself in our shoes and suggest a solution."

"Frankly, I've never given this any deep thought. But if you want my opinion, then revolt seems the best answer. If people cannot understand us, why be so keen to understand them?"

Nikhil listened in silence while I did the talking for both of us. "Rati, I've thought about it a lot and I have another answer, weird and eccentric, but not to be written off completely."

I could see she was interested. Taking a sip of coffee she said, "I'm eager to learn what you've come up with."

"Conditional marriage – where you are independent to live your life and your spouse is not obliged to follow the set rules of marriage either. No physical and emotional connect."

She looked at me, her deep brown eyes steady on my face. "Anuj, it's easy to concoct these things over coffee but they are very difficult to execute. Finding a partner for such a marriage will in itself be quite a task."

There was silence as we gazed into our coffee cups. Then I said baldly, "You could be our scapegoat and we yours."

There was a startled look on Rati's face. For the first time since we had sat down I saw a break in her composure.

"Sorry…I didn't get that," she said.

"See Rati, let's work out an arrangement. If you marry Nikhil, it will give you both the 'straight' label. You will be Nikhil's shield and he yours. To the world you will be husband and wife, but privately, you will both be able to live the life you have chosen," I elucidated.

Rati was rattled. "I have one word for such a conditional stand, and that is 'rubbish'! We don't even know each other Anuj and you are asking me to be a part of this grand plan to save your boyfriend from his mother? He should rather have the spine to face her."

"Have *you* told your parents or has your girlfriend done so?" Nikhil asked in a calm and composed manner.

She was left speechless. She had not, nor did she have plans to do so in the future.

"Look Rati, this arrangement can solve all our problems. I'm sure you must be facing a similar issue," I said.

"I am; everyone does for that matter," she replied in a practical tone.

"I want you to think it over. It's a win-win for both sides." My voice sounded convincing, even to my own ears.

"It is a big thing, Anuj. I will consult Niharika before taking a decision. I hope you have a role for Niharika and yourself planned as well in all this?"

I knew what she was referring to. I smiled and nodded. "She must of course be a close confidante. But I would like to know your first views on the proposal."

"Anuj, first I'd really like to get to know you both and reassure myself before taking any decision. For instance, if I enter into this arrangement, all you want from me is to fake a relationship with Nikhil?"

"Right, fake a relationship. All we need to do is help each other survive the journey and emerge at the other end with what we want."

"I don't know what to say or think; it's so sudden and surprising. I'll talk to Niharika," Rati said, taking a sip.

***

And so we gave ourselves time to construct the whole scenario. We had to make it a safe arrangement for all of us. It took quite a while for things to shape up at Rati's end and we often met during this time. The more I met her the more I learnt about her. She was trustworthy and came from a good family background. The thing that worked in Nikhil and my favour was that Rati had even more to fear, making it easier for us. Niharika, Rati's partner, hailed from a middle class family and she worked in an IT firm. They had met on Facebook, using fake IDs to get into a relationship. While Niharika had quite a history of relationships, for Rati it had been a first. Now they were deeply and quietly committed to each other.

Listening to Rati tell their simple story, I reflected on the tangled web of our relationships and thought of Martin Luther King's words: *The Negro needs the white man to free him from his fears. The white man needs the Negro to free him from his guilt.*

***

Rati and Nikhil agreed to marry on a private understanding that they would separate in due course and then divorce, stating incompatibility and irreconciliable differences. The joke only the four of us share is that we will all go on a honeymoon together – Nikhil and I, Rati and Niharika.

The arrangement works for us. We are happy living two lives – one for ourselves, confined to my little apartment, and one for the world, Nikhil's mother, Rati's parents, and all the rest – that's our second, larger, more true yet less complete life.

Nikhil has changed too. No longer overtly romantic or lost in boring activities, he has become more balanced, as if he has let go of something. I breathed an inward sigh of relief.

"I feel happy about how things are turning out for all of us," I say to him in a carefree voice. I too, had changed somewhere along the way from the naïve ardent lad I once was.

"It was your idea," Nikhil smiles, reducing the volume of the sound system. "So, anything else on your mind?"

"Nothing in particular. I am merely basking in the sunshine of happiness and contentment. We will think when it is time to think."

His lips curl in a reluctant smile. "Everyone needs a person like you in their life, someone whom they can love and depend on."

My inner goddess nods in frantic agreement, dancing in joyful abandon.

***

After days we are together again. Nikhil takes his place on the couch while I prepare the drinks. He is busy on his mobile, staring at spreadsheets. I glance at him – still the same marvel I met six years ago. So much has changed since then, so much that we have changed for ourselves.

"Drinks," I announce.

"Yeah," he mumbles, his eyes still on the spreadsheets. "How do such idiotic people reach such high positions?"

"Don't mess up your mind with such thoughts at this hour. It's time to relax, have a drink and find peace with me. Sleep with good thoughts, you can work tomorrow. So baby, it's time to put your lovely gadget out of reach." I take his phone from him and place it on the table.

He sits back with a sigh, saying, "I accept."

I drop down beside him and raise my lips to meet his. Wildfire spreads through my veins; my body is seized with joy. My fingers curl in his hair as he pushes me down on the sofa. I can feel his need, he can feel my passion.

We make each other complete.

*****

I read an article on the mass shooting at a gay bar in Orlando, USA – yet another example of anti-gay bigotry in the world. Probably inspired by homophobia, it was the worst mass-shooting in America, with over 50 people gunned down. But if it was indeed homophobia, it did not emerge from a vacuum; it was deeply rooted in the way modern society has shaped itself.

The year 2015 was a phenomenal one in the history of LGBT rights, when the Obama Administration put its weight behind the legalization of gay marriages. At the same time, a rancorous atmosphere was created by American religious groups to oppose the move. The Baptist Church held public protests proclaiming 'God hates fags', supported by the Republican Party, portraying the LGBT community as sinful deviants.

This is the usual picture not just in America but around the world. In the US and European nations, at least homosexuality is not criminalized the way it is in India and some Islamic nations. In India there is a religio-political stand against LGBT rights but anti-gay bigotry exists in every corner of the world. The danger of homophobia bubbles just under the surface. Gay men have been thrown from heights into baying crowds in Syria, chained and beaten to death in the name of executing sodomites, chased off cliffs by their own families, and many a time been compelled to commit suicide, not able to take the hate anymore. The madness is never too far away, either you take it and live it or you wear a mask to hide behind.

The shooting in Orlando holds clues for us in India. Unless we change our archaic laws, which deny not just liberty but also debar gays from proper medical treatment, and adopt more liberal views on homosexuality, there will always be a radical time bomb ticking. India, once the most sexually liberated of nations in ancient times, embracing the spectrum of human sexuality, now sighs under the political and social clamour surrounding homosexuality.

Recently, Congress Member of Parliament Shashi Tharoor, was prevented from introducing a Bill attacking Section 377 in the Indian Parliament. Either the political class does not consider this an issue important enough to be discussed in Parliament or they are simply afraid of the fallout in striking down Section 377. Perhaps both.

In July 2009, when the Delhi High Court struck down Section 377, which criminalizes non-penile, non-vaginal sex, activists called it historic. They had long argued that Section 377 is in dissonance with the right to privacy, dignity, life and liberty, the right to sexual expression, sexual preferences and even the moral right of association. While the State chose not to appeal, religious groups opposed the judgement. The verdict was reversed by the Supreme Court, but in the intervening years, the closeted tasted freedom for the first time, and society grew more aware and tolerant of LGBT rights.

There is no going back. The *joie de vivre* on streets of Mumbai, Delhi, Kolkata and even the small cities, was an indicator of social acceptance however much the law lags behind in creating an inclusive India. This acceptance has come just in time for the younger generations who are willing to break out of stereotypical social structures. Several Indian cities have seen 'queer freedom' marches; Indians have started talking about the issue, movies have been made using homosexuality as a central theme and articles have been written. The masses have shown support to pride moments on social networks.

It's a juggling act—accommodating others, opening up to parents, and accepting oneself as one is. It takes a very long time to create public consciousness in India, riddled as it is with odious socio-religious attitudes. Gays in India find many reasons to remain closeted – family attitudes, societal pressure, job security and even shame and guilt. There is no gay icon, no celebrity or leader who has taken a firm stand on homosexuality. The vast majority decide to get married and often end by ruining lives. Living as partners is difficult after a certain age as society considers it its right to question one's marital status. Knowing everyone's business is a national imperative in India.

I don't exactly remember what made me condense this theme for my debut novel. Gay fiction is seen more as advocacy than literature in our country. My friends were shattered by the idea and strongly urged me to rethink. More surprising were their reactions. *Indian and gay don't have novelty value* was one blunt comment. Some even asked me about my sexual orientation.

However, I proceeded with the idea and researched the topic.

The more I talked with people, the more I could feel the deep fear, profound self-doubt and inability to peacefully enjoy a family life. Some had been harassed, abused, cheated and made to do things they would never have done in the normal course. Most were uncertain about their future, fearing to open up to their families. Some had even thought of committing suicide. I lent my ear to many painful stories about lives ruined by the sheer fear of coming out of closet.

The entire journey of writing this book on this theme has taken me deep into depths I would have never have otherwise dived into. In searching for the truth I initiated conversations I might never have done on a subject I might never have cared about. In making these attempts to absorb the reality of a socially disenfranchised community, I have seen hopes die, experienced growing indifference and contempt, but at times I have seen the glimmer of the Morning Star, growing more visible. I can see the hope of society becoming more tolerant. It remains for the judiciary to repair the injustice and damage they have done to millions through their judgements.

*****

ACKNOWLEDGEMENTS

I always wanted to lead a life reading books – learning from the plots, getting immersed in the narration, living the emotions, flipping pages. I read to live, to condense my life to a drop of essence. I never realized that while I read, the writer in me was getting trained. I started concocting plots while attending meetings and through dialogues on bus and metro rides. Observing people became a habit. I felt a calling. One day I got down to putting thoughts on paper. The first page of my story was written. The momentum could not have been sustained had it not been for the wonderful people around me. There was always someone I could go to and chat with when I needed motivation to go on:

My family – my loving parents, caring brother and sister-in-law, for their faith in. Thanks also to my aunt Meenu Mehrotra, for her continuous guidance and encouragement.

My super-great friends – Pragya, Richa and Leena, for continuously pushing me towards my goal and for sitting for hours listening to my plot over coffee (often paid for or made by them). I owe much to these ladies. Their silent leanings, *'wow'* *'really'* *'naah'* *'that is much better'* meant a lot.

Thanks also to Vikram, for continuously encouraging me with stories and for being a spiritual guide during the most difficult phase of the journey.

Thanks to the editorial team for pouring in a lot of thought to bring the wanted balance between literature and philosophy in the story and ensuring that the essence of relationships and sensitivity of the matter is not lost in narratives.

And big thanks to all the nameless, often faceless, guys who believed in me and shared their stories. I often felt unsure about writing on this sensitive topic but their stories, the half smiles, tears, unfinished sentences and the agony of deeply inflicted wounds, kept me going. Thanks for being part of the research and truth, shaped here as fiction.

*****

www.ingramcontent.com/pod-product-compliance
Lightning Source LLC
Chambersburg PA
CBHW021142260726
48656CB00024B/1189